The
Nature Parks
of
FRANCE

The Author
Patrick Delaforce already has twenty-two books to his name, including travel guides and books on the wine regions of France. For many years he lived in the heart of the French countryside and is a frequent visitor to the Nature Parks.

Credits
Front cover photograph of Chamois by G. Lombart, PN Mercantour; Back cover, top: PNR de la Haute-Vallée de Chevreuse; middle: PNR de la Brenne; bottom: PNR du Nord/Pas de Calais. All illustrations courtesy of the French National Tourist Office, London and various Parcs Naturels Régionals. Thanks also to the Fédération des Parcs Naturels de France, Paris.

Index by Gillian Delaforce
Cover design by Zeebra

Notes to the reader
1. Symbols used in the maps are:
     ✳ Maison du Parc
     𝑖 Tourist office
2. *Syndicats d'Initiatives* (abbreviation: SIs). This is the name given to smaller tourist offices; they are normally open 1000–1230, 1500–1900 in season only.
3. *Museums*. Most museums charge a small fee. Usual entry hours are 0900–1200, 1400–1900. They are often closed on Tuesdays.

The
Nature Parks
of
FRANCE

Patrick Delaforce

THE WINDRUSH PRESS • GLOUCESTERSHIRE

First published in Great Britain by
The Windrush Press
Little Window,
High Street, Moreton-in-Marsh,
Gloucestershire GL56 0LL
Telephone 01608 652012
Fax: 01608 652125

British Library Cataloguing-in-Publication Data
A catalogue reference for this book is available from the British Library

ISBN 0 900075 93 7

Printed and bound in Great Britain by Bell & Bain Ltd, Glasgow

CONTENTS

CONTENTS

INTRODUCTION

The majority of British travellers would probably nominate France as the most beautiful country in Europe. A large country of nearly 550,000 square kilometres, it lies at the centre of western Europe and has a lengthy coastline, fed by a dozen famous rivers, and superb mountain ranges along the eastern and southern borders. Because the autoroute network is now so comprehensive, it is very easy to overlook the beauties of the countryside. The 32 national and regional nature parks are off the beaten track in the *arrière pays* and are therefore not often visited. The best known is La Camargue in southern Provence, famous for its white horses, black fighting bulls, pink flamingos, gypsies, mosquitoes and beetles! Because of their relative inaccessibility these beautiful *espaces vertes* have rarely been documented in the English language.

It is perhaps rather surprising that *la belle France* did not introduce its initial legislation for the creation of its national parks until 22 July 1960. Similar parks had existed in neighbouring Germany since 1909 and in Italy since 1922. The six national parks – Cévennes, Écrins, Mercantour, Pyrénées, Vanoise and Port-Cros – cover 2 per cent of the national land area, are open to the public and usually have no roads. The populations are sparse, and the state is responsible through a director and staff for the protection of the flora and fauna of the local landscape against outside harmful influences. Tourist facilities are provided for the 4 million people who visit each year. The national parks are public institutions with operating expenses borne by the Ministry of the Environment. Staff numbers in the parks vary from 24 to 70. In the central core of each national park there is a ban on hunting activities, camping, building and road construction. Access is often difficult, but the rewards are considerable. The small colony of wild bears in the Pyrénées is well protected. Ibex in the Mercantour have increased from 30 in 1963 to nearly 1000 today, and chamois from 400

1

to over 5000. The tawny vultures and beavers in the Cévennes have flourished notably, as have ibex in the Vanoise and seals in the underwater park of Port-Cros. A number of parks are twinned with their natural partners in Italy, Spain, Germany, Canada and Greece. More recently the European Community has encouraged twinning between British and French parks (see page 4).

Since a decree of 1 March 1967 was signed, 26 regional nature parks have been established. They account for 8 per cent of the national land mass and are members of the Paris-based Fédération des Parcs Naturels de France, founded in 1972. They have the same objectives as the national parks (nature conservation in traditional landscapes, the provision of tourist facilities) but are funded by the Ministry of the Environment (13 per cent), local communes (20 per cent), the *départements* (27 per cent) and regional authorities (40 per cent). In addition economic activities within the parks are encouraged, provided they are compatible with protection of the environment. Nearly 2000 communes with 2 million inhabitants are to be found within the regional parks.

A glance at the map on page 3 will show that the parks are widely dispersed and vary enormously in style – from mountain ranges, densely forested plains and wetlands to offshore reserves, such as Port-Cros and L'Armorique in Brittany, which includes sea-girt islands. The four most popular sites, which are therefore overcrowded in midsummer, are the Vallée des Merveilles in the Parc de Mercantour, the Sommet du Puy-de-Dôme in the Parc des Volcans d'Auvergne, Cap Blanc-Nez in the Parc Nord/Pas-de-Calais and the Col du Lautaret in the Parc National des Écrins. So it would help protect the French ecology if you visited out of season!

This book has been written specifically for the relatively 'green' and environmentally conscious traveller, perhaps with a family, as children will undoubtedly be interested. Each park is documented in the same format and practical information and suggestions are included such as: approach roads, main characteristics, location of Park HQ, vegetation, fauna, local walks, places to stay, what to see and what to do. They are presented in a clockwise pattern so that a batch of three or four can be fitted into a week's visit.

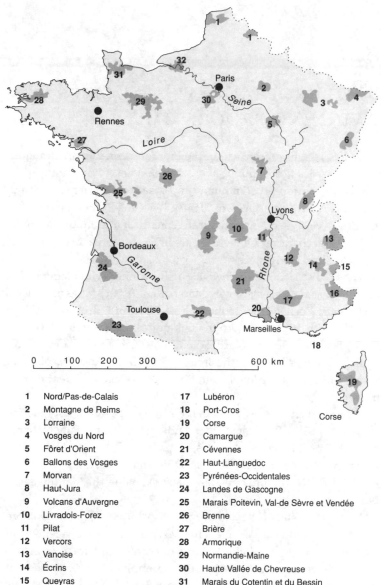

1	Nord/Pas-de-Calais	**17**	Lubéron
2	Montagne de Reims	**18**	Port-Cros
3	Lorraine	**19**	Corse
4	Vosges du Nord	**20**	Camargue
5	Fôret d'Orient	**21**	Cévennes
6	Ballons des Vosges	**22**	Haut-Languedoc
7	Morvan	**23**	Pyrénées-Occidentales
8	Haut-Jura	**24**	Landes de Gascogne
9	Volcans d'Auvergne	**25**	Marais Poitevin, Val-de-Sèvre et Vendée
10	Livradois-Forez	**26**	Brenne
11	Pilat	**27**	Brière
12	Vercors	**28**	Armorique
13	Vanoise	**29**	Normandie-Maine
14	Écrins	**30**	Haute Vallée de Chevreuse
15	Queyras	**31**	Marais du Cotentin et du Bessin
16	Mercantour	**32**	Brotonne

THE EUROPEAN NATURAL SITES TWINNING PROGRAMME

After 1987, the European Year of the Environment, Eurosite, an international association of public and private bodies, was created. Sponsored by the European Community and based on Lille, it manages and encourages the European Natural Sites Twinning Programme. To date 41 sites have signed twinning arrangements of a technical, scientific and cultural character. Of these six are in England, two in Ireland and no fewer than 14 in France.

The English sites are: Titchwell Marsh (twinned with Platier d'Oye in Nord/Pas-de-Calais); Elmley Marsh, Kent (with Marais et Vasières Charentais, Rochefort, near the Marais Poitevin); Strumpshaw Fen, Norfolk (with the Réserve Ornithologique de la Gabrière, in the Brenne PNR); Beaulieu Estuary, North Solent (with Estuaire de l'Orne, Normandy); Ranworth Staithe, the Broads (with Marais Audomarois); and Somerset Levels and Moors (with PNR des Marais du Cotentin et du Bessin).

Other French sites involved in the *jumelage*/twinning programme are: Les Sept-Iles, Britanny; Baie d'Audierne, Britanny; Parc National de Port-Cros; Massif des Agriates, Corsica; La Palissade, Camargue; Le Teich, PNR des Landes de Gascogne; Embouchure de la Canche, south of PNR du Nord/Pas-de-Calais; Domaine du Marquenterre, Baie de Somme, Picardy.

Most of the sites are visited by migratory birds and are rich in flora and fauna. Technical information is exchanged on management of reedbeds, aquatic vegetation, dune protection and habitat improvement through grazing. Some practical examples of work carried out include research into the disappearance of Bewick swans in the Marais Contentin and the corncrake in the Somerset Levels and Moors.

NORD/PAS-DE-CALAIS

Region: ARTOIS/FLANDERS

Among the battlefields of World War I and World War II, between the large industrial cities of the northeast, nestling in the sombre region of declining mines and tips, are – surprisingly – three substantial green lungs that form this unusual park. In 1968 the first nature park in France was created – the St-Amand-Raismes park of 10,000 ha which is between Valenciennes and Lille. Ten years later it became part of the much larger Nord/Pas-de-Calais park of 167,000 ha with 202 communes and 314,000 inhabitants. Few arrivals by ferry at Calais or Boulogne or by the new Channel tunnel will realise that a large nature park is within walking distance.

The western area is called Le Boulonnais and, as the name suggests, surrounds Boulogne, extending 15 km south, nearly 25 km north to Sangatte and the Chunnel terminal, and from up to 30 km inland. A flat land, it is watered by the rivers Liane, Wimereux and Slack, and there are several forests – Hardelot, Desvres, Boulogne and Guînes – *bocages* and market gardens. Between the small *plage* towns along the coast, between the sandy beaches and dunes, lie two very popular, often over-visited capes, Blanc-Nez and Gris-Nez, with magnificent birdlife and views of La Manche.

The second park area is reached from Boulogne by the N42, with Lumbres to the west and St-Omer and Arques to the east. It is called L'Audomarois et les Monts de Flandre and has a large *marais*, lakes, the river Aa, and the forests of Tournehem, Éperlecques, Ham and Clairmarais.

The third park area, La Plaine de la Scarpe et de l'Escaut, is much further inland and is reached by the A23 from Lille or Dunkerque or by the N45 from Douai or Arras. It is just to the north of Valenciennes and it has the Forêt de Raismes-St-Amand-Wallers at its heart. The rivers Scarpe and Escaut go through the park which also contains the lakes of Condé-sur-l'Escaut, Hergnies and La Mare à Goriaux. An unusually wide variety of fauna can be seen in the marshlands beside the canals.

A determined effort has been made by the authorities to encourage the ecological protection of this large, not very interesting industrial

5

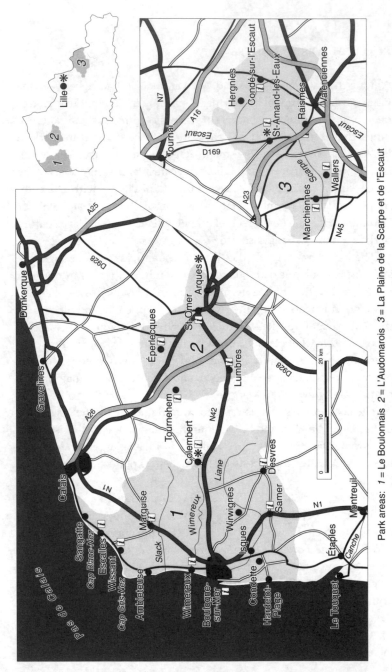

Park areas: *1* = Le Boulonnais *2* = L'Audomarois *3* = La Plaine de la Scarpe et de l'Escaut

area by introducing an extensive educational programme for young children. Botanical and ornithological visits and studies are organised throughout the year. Adults, however, are not forgotten. The last weekend in September sees a multi-activity *fête* and fair across the area which attracts over 100,000 visitors. Altogether the park receives over 3 million visitors each year.

Maps. Michelin 51, 53; IGN 1, 2, 101.

Access. The A26 starts at Calais to the north of the Boulonnais and goes through the Audomarois. The A25 begins south of Dunkerque and southeast of Lille joins the A23, which runs through the Plaine de la Scarpe et de l'Escaut. There are SNCF stations at Calais, Boulogne, St-Omer and Valenciennes, and local buses radiate outwards from those four towns. Airports are at Le Touquet, Marck/Calais and Wisques/St-Omer.

Park HQ. For the park as a whole the head office is Espace Naturel Régional, 17 rue Jean-Roisin, 59800 Lille (☎ 20.60.60.60). It is more practical, however, to consult the area HQs which are:

Boulonnais. Manoir de Huisbois, Le Wast, 62142 Colembert (☎ 21.33.38.79). Reached by N42 east from Boulogne, then left and north 1 km on D127.

Audomarois. Le Grand Vannage, Les Quatres Faces, 62510 Arques (☎ 21.98.62.98). Reached by N42 east from St-Omer.

Plaine de la Scarpe et de l'Escaut. Le Luron, 357 rue Notre-Dame-d'Amour, 59230 St-Amand-les-Eaux (☎ 27.48.78.77). Reached by D169 from Valenciennes past Raismes.

Each of the three areas also has information offices – 18 altogether.

FAUNA

In the Rond de la Fontaine Bouillon in the forest of Raismes is a *parc animalier* of 104 ha, where wild boar, wild sheep (*mouflon*), fallow deer, stags and hinds roam freely (open Mar.–Oct.). Nearby is La Mare à Goriaux, where in summer one can see 200 bird species including tufted grebe, spoonbill duck, teal, pochard, black coot, sedge warbler and many other avifauna. In the central area of the Audomarois on the lakes of Romalaere (3 km from St-Omer by D209) can be seen reed

7

buzzard, yellowhammer, owl, wren, tomtit, great tit, willow-warbler, coot, moorhen and, particularly, grey heron. But birdwatchers would be better rewarded on the Boulonnais coast – Caps Gris-Nez and Blanc-Nez, Platier d'Oye near Gravelines, the Embouchure de la Canche near Le Touquet, and further south the Parc Ornithologique du Marquenterre northwest of Abbeville. Silver gull, jackdaw, kestrel, housemartin, swallow and stormy petrel can be seen at Cap Blanc-Nez. Eider duck, seamew, button-quail, oyster-catcher, magpie, violet sand-piper, turnstone, pipit and many others at Cap Gris-Nez. The Marquenterre reserve, an important wetland known as the Camargue of the North, is a vast area of saltings and brackish grassland similar to the Dutch polders with dunes often reaching a height of 40 m. Many migrant waders and wildfowl have been recorded including grey plover, scaup, bar-tailed godwit, brent goose, osprey and egret. Breeding species include avocet, white stork, spoonbill, Kentish plover, greylag goose, shelduck and many others. In and around the canals and waterways are polecat, muskrat and fox. And of course there are salt-water fish and shellfish from the coastal ports, and freshwater fish in the dozen rivers.

FLORA AND VEGETATION

In the habitats of reclaimed mining land, bogs and marshes, dunes and chalk grasslands there are also many forests. The Forêt de Raismes-St-Amand-Wallers has 5000 ha of oak, beech, birch and poplar. Along the rivers are to be seen willow, poplar and alder. The coastal sand-dune vegetation consists of marram grass, lyme grass and sea buckthorn, although maritime pine has been planted to stabilise the sand in some areas. The Office National des Forêts (☎ 27.26.61.55) offers study walks to inspect local flora.

WHAT TO DO

Walks. The Grande Randonnée du Littoral and the GR 121 follow the coastline north–south from Dunkerque, Calais, Boulogne and Le Touquet inland to Montreuil. The GR 120 also follows the coastline but a few km inland, through the Forêt de Guînes, Forêt de Boulogne, Forêt de Desvres, and southwards. Deviations such as the GR 127 and 129 are mainly in a west–east direction. The GR 128 goes through the Audomarois sector of the park. And in the eastern park area the GR

121 reappears. For local walks ask for a *sentiers* plan from the local Park HQ. There are five in the Plaine de la Scarpe et de l'Escaut, another five in the Audomarois and nine in the Boulonnais.

Horse-riding. In the Boulonnais *centres équestres* are at Wirwignes, Condette, Hardelot, Isques, Nabringhen and Wimereux.

In the Plaine de la Scarpe et de l'Escaut there are six in Raismes-St-Amand-Wallers, with others at St-Amand-les-Eaux and Beuvry-la-Forêt.

Cycling/VTT (*vélos tout terrain*). In Boulonnais cycle rental in Boulogne at SNCF station and at youth hostel, rue de la Porte-Gayole; Desvres at campsite, bd Clocherville; Hardelot at SNCF; Marquise, 19 rue de Verdun; Wierre-Effroy; Wimereux. In Audomarois rental at SNCF St-Omer; Salperwick. In Plaine de la Scarpe et de l'Escaut rental at SNCF St-Amand and Gîte du Liron.

Canoe/kayak. Boulonnais: Boulogne at 7 bd Chanzy. Audomarois: St-Omer, consult tourist office. Plaine de la Scarpe et de l'Escaut: two rentals outside Valenciennes at Étang du Vignoble.

Canal boating. A range of boats can be hired or cruises arranged along the 680 km of canals, through Association Tourisme Fluvial, BP 46, 59426 Armentières (☎ 20.35.29.07). Also Marais Audomarois, St-Omer (☎ 21.98.66.74).

Sports. Sailboarding, sailing, archery, fishing, etc. Consult Park HQ.

Spa treatment. At St-Amand-les-Eaux are a thermal spa, grand hotel and casino set in a large park. The hydrotherapy may do wonders for sciatica and rheumatism.

WHAT TO SEE

Châteaux. Condé-sur-l'Escaut, northeast of Valenciennes, has two châteaux. In the Boulonnais, Hardelot, Wierre-au-Bois, Bellebrune and Boulogne (Pont-de-Briques, Aumont) all have châteaux.

Churches. There is the basilica at Boulogne, the Abbaye St-Paul at

9

Wisques/St-Omer, the Basilica Notre-Dame at St-Omer and the abbey at St-Amand-les-Eaux where there are carillon concerts.

Sangatte Eurotunnel. The French end of the Channel tunnel. Centre d'Information ☎ 21.46.41.58.

World War II sites. At Landrethin/Marquise there is a V3 base in Mimoyecques fort; Éperlecques Blockhaus, northwest of St-Omer, housed a V2 base; Ambleteuse, north of Boulogne, has a collection of arms and uniforms in Fort Vauban, as does Audinghen/Wissant.

Ecological activities. At Centre d'Amaury near Hergnies north of Valenciennes; at Étaples near Le Touquet is La Maison de la Faune et de la Flore in Clos St-Victor; and at Claimarais east of St-Omer is the Grange-Nature with flora and fauna exhibitions.

Museums. At Guînes Musée Émile-Villez, local history; at St-Omer Beaux-Arts in Hôtel Sanderlin and Musée Henri-Dupuis, ornithological collection; Boulogne has the museums of Centre National de la Mer showing local maritime traditions and the Beaux-Arts in the Château-Musée. At Desvres east of Boulogne is the ceramics Maison de la Faïence. At Escalles southwest of Calais is submarine geology in Musée du Transmanche. In Hydrequent/Rinxent northeast of Boulogne is the Musée du Marbre et Géologie. Samer southeast of Boulogne has works by the local painter Cazin; and in St-Amand-les-Eaux northwest of Valenciennes is a ceramics and *beaux-arts* museum.

WHERE TO STAY

Youth hostels are to be found in Anzin (surburb of Valenciennes), Boulogne, Montreuil and Dunkerque. Along the Grandes Randonnées 121, 122 and 129 are 27 *gîtes d'étape*, and within the park are 100 campsites. Ask for list from tourist offices.

TOURIST OFFICES

Boulonnais. At Escalles, Wimereux, Marquise, Colembert, Boulogne, Desvres, Ambleteuse, Wissant and Samer.
Audomarois. At Tournehem, Éperlecques, St-Omer and Lumbres.

Plaine de la Scarpe et de l'Escaut. At St-Amand-les-Eaux, Condé-sur-l'Escaut, Raismes, Wallers and Marchiennes.

MONTAGNE DE REIMS
Region: CHAMPAGNE

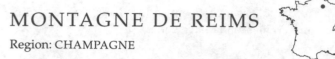

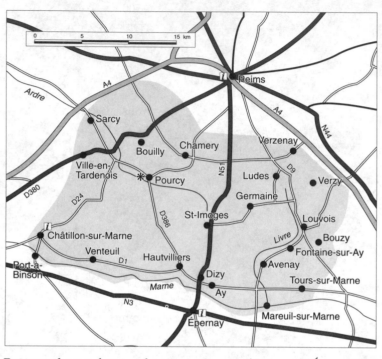

Between the two famous champagne towns of Reims and Épernay lies the smallish nature park of La Montagne de Reims. Founded in 1975, it has 68 communes with 36,000 inhabitants in the Marne *département*, which suffered so badly in World War I. The area of the park extends to 50,000 ha, of which 20,000 ha are forest, 23,000 ha cultivated land and, rare for a nature park, 7000 ha prime vineyards. This sandstone massif area is covered with small lakes and has the attractive river Marne flowing east–west from Châlons-sur-Marne past Épernay to Château-Thierry forming the southern boundary of the park. The river Ardre rises near Mont Joli and feeds into the river Vesle at Fismes, and the Livre, a small tributary of the Marne, rises near the Maison du Bucheron at Germaine. The mountain peaks are Mont Sinai at 283 m and Mont Joli at 274 m. For wine-lovers there is an interesting cham-

12

pagne route taking in half a dozen small but well-known villages such as Ay, Hautvilliers and Bouzy. Apart from wine cultivation, agriculture and forestry are important. There are châteaux, museums, good walks and many interesting visits outside the park perimeter. One unique feature is strange, twisted beech trees – some 500 years old – called Les Faux de Verzy, in the northeast sector of the park.

Maps. Michelin 56; IGN 9, 10.

Access. Between Reims and Épernay by N51. Westwards from Châlons-sur-Marne by D1 to Ay, eastwards from Château-Thierry also by D1. The D1 and N3 run close and parallel to the river Marne, but the first is recommended since it passes through many of the champagne wine villages. The minor roads D24, D386 and D9 run north–south through the park. The autoroute A4 runs through Reims along the northern boundary. The SNCF service travels through the park from Reims to Épernay stopping at Rilly, Germaine, Avenay and Ay. Bus services from the two main towns run to the rural areas of the park. There are airports at Reims and Épernay.

Park HQ. In modern buildings, the Maison du Parc is not easy to find. It is just outside the village of Pourcy on the D386 19 km northwest of Épernay near a World War I German/British cemetery. It offers a wide range of tourist and ecological advice provided you can find it! (☎ 26.59.44.44.) 0830–1800, closed weekends.

FAUNA

The park authorities have made a determined effort to protect the wild boar (*sanglier*)population despite the ambitions of hungry local sportsmen. There is the traditional woodland fauna of red and roe deer, fox, hare and rabbits, but only basic birdlife.

FLORA AND VEGETATION

The woods in the centre of the park have many tree varieties including hornbeam, chestnut, silver pine, birch, willow and poplar, as well as the 650 peculiar twisted beech trees called Les Faux de Verzy. There are many flowers in the woodlands and along the road verges, including campanula, cornflower, iris, valerian, sage, poppy, marguerite, glasswort and the occasional orchid. The vineyards are along the southern slopes of the massif, and the 7000 ha include some famous growers.

WHAT TO DO

Walks. The Grande Randonnée 14 comes from the west just north of the river Marne into Ay where the GR 141 joins and both lead northeast about 10 km apart towards Verzy. The GR 142 starts in the northwest at Fismes and goes through Ville-en-Tardenois south to Châtillon-sur-Marne. The Park HQ has a leaflet with 12 suggested local walks.

Horse-riding. *Centres équestres* are at Sarcy, Chamery and Parc du Château St-Martin-d'Ablois.

Cycling/VTT. Hire from Avenay-Val-d'Or, Fontaine-sur-Ay, Tauxière, Ay and St-Imoges. Also SNCF stations at Reims, Épernay and Châlons-sur-Marne will rent cycles. Ask the Park HQ for a list of suggested itineraries.

Canoe/kayak. Several villages along the river Marne rent out canoes. Details from tourist offices. There are *centres nautiques* at Dormans, Tours-sur-Marne and Port-à-Binson.

Archery. *Tir à l'arc* at Villers-sous-Châtillon.

Caving/fishing. Ask Park HQ for leaflets.

Boat trips. The good ship *La Champagne* at Cumières *embarcadère* just west of Dizy on the D1 cruises down the river Marne. The office is at 15 pl. de la République, Épernay (☎ 26.54.49.51). There are visits by boat or boat/walk to explore the wine villages. Also 1½ hour walking tours of *Faune et Flore* from rail station at Épernay.

Wine tours. Apart from Les Grandes Marques – internationally well known – with extensive *chais* (cellars) in Reims or Épernay, there are 30 or more relatively unknown shippers in the wine villages who will be delighted to see you, arrange a tasting and rely on you to buy some bottles. Try Bouzy, home of red (not pink) champagne. Ask at tourist offices for their advice and perhaps telephone to make an appointment.

WHAT TO SEE

Châteaux. La Malmaison at Ay; Mareuil-sur-Ay (18thC); Château Louvois; Château du Breuil at Avenay-Val-d'Or; Château de Boursault near Venteuil south of the river; and Vandières (11–18thC).

Abbey of Hautvilliers. The 16–18thC abbey in the village where Dom Pérignon, the cellarer, discovered secondary fermentation and effervescence! The abbey was unfortunately burned by English troops in the 16thC but has been lovingly restored.

Churches. Ay; Bisseul; Ambonnay; Avenay-Val-d'Or; Venteuil, which has a monument to the British World War I dead; 12thC Revil; the Abbaye de l'Amour-Dieu at Troissy; the 12thC priory at Binzon; 12thC Damery; and the 12–16thC Chapelle Ste-Lie at Ville-Dommange.

Maison du Vigneron. The small winemakers' museum at St-Imoges.

Maison du Boucheron at Germaine. Open weekends 1430–1830 Apr.–Nov. A permanent exhibition of folklore and traditions of forestry workers. The source of the river Livre is a few hundred metres away.

Domaine de Commetreuil at Bouilly. A centre for forest exploration and walks (150 ha), orienteering, nature and botany studies. Telephone Park HQ.

Craft centre at Ville-en-Tardenois northwest on the D380. Apr.–Nov. ulleiiuiiini A wide range of local activities, also a *gîte d'étape* for 15 people.

Observatory on Mont Sinai. Panorama from Tour Brisset near Louvois.

Windmill at Verzenay overlooking the vineyards in the northeast corner.

Canal Latéral de la Marne. The 19thC canal on the east side of the park has been cleared and planted with 1200 trees along 8 km.

15

Festivals. There are 40 brotherhoods of St Vincent, patron saint of Champenois vineyards, who have their own *ecomusée* and sponsor vignerons' *fêtes* in the wine villages, including Ambonnay. Ask tourist offices for details of *fêtes, foires*, etc.

WHERE TO STAY

There are campsites at Dormans, Épernay, Mareuil-le-Port, Villers-sous-Châtillon and Port-à-Binson. There is a youth hostel at Verzy, nine *gîtes d'étape* and a dozen *gîtes* and *chambres d'hôte*. Ask for the list from Épernay tourist office. Some of the wine-growing villages have small *auberges* and Épernay has a good range of hotels.

TOURIST OFFICES

Épernay. 7 ave. de Champagne (☎ 26.55.33.00).
Châlons-sur-Marne. Pl. Godard (☎ 26.65.17.89).
Reims. 1 rue Jadart (☎ 26.47.25.69).
Châtillon-sur-Marne. 11 rue de l'Église (☎ 26.58.34.66).
Dormans. Mairie, rue du Pont (☎ 26.58.21.45).

REGIONAL VISITS

Reims. Visit cathedral, Basilique St-Rémi, three museums and many famous wine-cellars.
Épernay. Visit four museums, 16thC Église St-Martin and still more famous wine-cellars.
Châlons-sur-Marne. See Cathédrale St-Étienne, Église Notre-Dame-en-Vaux, Église St-Alpin, three museums.

World War I guided tours include Fort de la Pompelle and the original trenches 5 km east of Reims.

LORRAINE

Region: LORRAINE

Founded in 1974, the Parc Naturel Régional de Lorraine occupies 206,000 ha with 205 communes and a population of 45,000. It is unusual in that roughly two-thirds of the park lies west of the road, rail and river Moselle links between the large cities of Metz and Nancy, while the remaining third forms a quite separate sector some 25 km to the east. The three *départements* concerned are Moselle, Meurthe-et-Moselle and Meuse. Both sectors are heavily wooded, with green rolling hills, farming pasturage and many large lakes. The river Moselle flowing through Metz and Pont-à-Mousson towards Nancy forms the eastern boundary of the western zone. And the river Meuse flowing through Verdun, St-Mihiel and Commercy towards Toul forms the western and southern boundaries. In the eastern sector two tributaries of the Moselle – the Sânon and Seille – are fed by the large lakes of Gondrexange, Stock, Lindre and Mittersheim. The rivers are navigable and are the scene of much nautical activity. There are few towns within the park. Pont-à-Mousson (pop. 16,000), where the Park HQ is situated, is on both banks of the Moselle halfway between Metz and Nancy and is technically just outside the western sector. A network of good roads within each sector makes travel easy to the many châteaux, museums, nature sites, churches, etc. Once the region was famous for its salt industry and even more famous for its terrible World War I battle-grounds, just east of Verdun on the N3. Now the park must be one of the most peaceful spots in France. Exotic wild flowers grow on the grassy sheltered limestone hills – *Petite Suisse Lorraine* is the name of one verdant corner – and over 300 varieties of birdlife can be seen on and around the lakes; fish are also plentiful. The casual visitor on the main intercity roads will miss these green spaces. Note the two zones are indicated below by the abbreviations WZ, EZ.

Maps. Michelin 57, 62; IGN 10, 11, 12.

Access
Western zone
From Verdun D964 south to Commercy and Toul. From Verdun east on

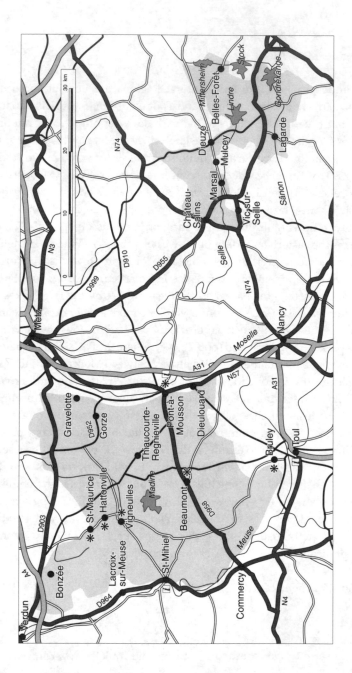

LORRAINE

N3 towards Metz. Metz–Pont-à-Mousson–Nancy by A31 or N57 or
D952. SNCF to Metz, Toul, Commercy and Nancy. Airports at Metz
and Nancy. There are many bus routes.

Eastern zone
From Metz southeast by D955 or D999 to Château-Salins or Dieuze.
From Nancy east by N74. SNCF rail Nancy–Château-Salins.

Park HQ. Located in a handsome manor house on the D952 on the west
bank of the river Moselle at Pont-à-Mousson, an industrial town:
Domaine de Charmilly, BP 35, chemin des Clos, 54702 Pont-à-Mousson
(☎ 83.81.11.91). It has produced a wide range of leaflets on practically
every subject. Other park information centres at Bruley, Beaumont,
Vigneulles, Hattonville and St-Maurice in WZ.

FAUNA

The park authorities have taken strong measures to protect the badger
colony in EZ. There are now about 200, averaging four per family and
doing well. Otter, wild boar, red deer and the unusual wild cat, which
can be seen in the nature reserve at Ste-Croix (EZ) and at Haye, just
west of Nancy, are among the indigenous animals. The park also
harbours 17 species of bat (*chauve-souris*). 120 migrating bird species
are noted around the lakes of Madine and Lachaussée (WZ), and a
recent survey showed 230 bird species around the Étang de Lindre
(EZ). The total 320 species include geese, grey and purple heron, rare
bittern, royal kite, pochard, black stork, white-tailed eagle, black-
winged stilt, collared flycatcher, golden oriole, grebe, duck and coot.
The park authorities have carefully rescued the diminishing species of
grey buzzard which nests in cornfields. Now 200 pairs fly freely thanks
to co-operation by local farmers. The park has also taken measures to
protect the sparrow-owl with 50 man-made nests in four park areas.
The Ste-Croix reserve has a colony of storks, and nightingales sing in
most of the woods. Freshwater fish – crayfish, carp, perch, pike and eel
– are found in the lakes and streams of Madine (1100 ha) and Lachaussée, both in WZ, and Lindre (630 ha) and Gondrexange in EZ.

The animal park of Ste-Croix (EZ) is open 1000–2000 (☎ 87.03.92.05).
Fee.

SALT MARSHES

Along the valley of the river Seille (EZ) are the Mares Salées, the salt marshes near Marsal (D38/D955). In the 14thC the Duke of Lorraine constructed a fortress at Château-Salins to protect the salt mines. Visit the Maison du Sel, Porte de France at Marsal (☎ 87.01.16.75). 1400–1800. Fee. See the machines, kilns, stoves and pumps in working condition.

FLORA AND VEGETATION

Oak, beech, birch, maple, ash, hawthorn and hazel are to be found in the main forests in WZ – Commercy, La Reine, La Montagne and Souilly – and in EZ – St-Jean, Bride and Fénétrange. Over 20 varieties of wild orchid are noted in May–Sept. and over 1100 species of flower and plant life have been counted in the park on a recent survey.

WHAT TO DO

Walks. There are over 1000 km of signed walks (*sentiers balisés*). The Grande Randonnée 5 starts in EZ at Gondrexange in the southeast corner (N4/D955 crossroads) goes north between lakes to Languimberg past the ornithological observatory south of Dieuze, and then west past Blanche-Église, Marsal and the salt marshes to Vic-sur-Seille. This is the western boundary of EZ. The GR 5 continues due west and crosses over the A31 and the river Moselle towards Liverdun, where it enters the eastern boundary of WZ. It heads northwest to Martincourt, just west of Pont-à-Mousson, crosses the Rupt de Mad and exits out of the northeast corner at Ars-sur-Moselle. The six regions of the park have produced their own little topoguide. The Côtes de Meuse in the northwest of WZ; the Toulois in the south of WZ; the Trois Vallées in the centre of WZ; the Mosellane in the northeast corner of WZ and northwest corner of EZ. Pays de Madine in the centre of WZ; and Pays de Chambley in the northwest corner of WZ.

Horse-riding. There are *centres équestres* at Dieuze and Château-Salins (EZ) and Commercy, La Madine/Nonsard and Fresnes-en-Woevre (WZ).

River tours. There are 700 km of rivers and canals in or around the park. Boat tours (from *Porte* or *Halte Fluviales*) can be made from Nancy, Metz,

Toul, St-Mihiel, Lacroix-sur-Meuse, Verdun and Pont-à-Mousson in WZ and from Lagarde and Dieuze in EZ.

Cycling/VTT. Cycles can be rented at Lagarde and Dieuze (EZ) and at St-Maurice, Bonzée and Beaumont (WZ).

Sailing/canoeing is possible on the lakes of Madine, Gondrexange and Mittersheim (EZ) and Colvert/Bonzée (northwest of WZ).

Leisure parks. A range of activities, ideal for children, from *bases de loisirs* at Bonzée, Sommedieu, Madine, St-Mihiel in WZ, and Mittersheim and Gondrexange in EZ.

WHAT TO SEE

Châteaux. Dieulouard (south of Pont-à-Mousson), Commercy (Château Stanislaus), Jaulny and Hattonchâtel, all four in WZ; and Réchicourt-le-Château in EZ. Opening times vary, so check with tourist offices. Fee.

Natural sights. Observatory of Guermange (EZ); salt marshes of Marsal (EZ); *pelouse calcaire* (limestone pasture) of Genicourt (northwest corner of WZ); and three recommended woodland walks called *sentiers forestiers* at Villecey-sur-Mad (northeast side of WZ), Guermange (EZ) and Mulcey (EZ).

Museums
Western zone
Lucey – Maison Lorraine de Polyculture.
Thiaucourt-Regnieville – military history.
Hattonchâtel – Musée Louise-Cottin (painter).
Gorze – religious and Roman history.
Hannonville-sous-les-Côtes – folklore.
Gravelotte – Franco-Prussian War museum.
Ville-sur-Yron – ecovillage.
Bonzée – environment
Eastern zone
Vic-sur-Seille – art and history.
Marsal – salt-working history.

21

Belles-Forêts – Maison du Clement, July–Aug.

Churches/chapels. At Commercy (Chapelle de Gevau), Buxières (Chapelle des Bures), Heudicourt (Chapelle Notre-Dame-de-Lourdes) in WZ: Gélucourt (Chapelle de Marimont, Chapelle des Templiers) in EZ. In Pont-à-Mousson is the 18thC Abbaye des Prémontrés, now used as a cultural centre.

Craft centres. The Maison de l'Artisanat at St-Maurice-sous-les-Côtes (☎ 29.89.38.95) is near the lake of Madine. Also visit Côtes de Toul near Bruley (WZ), a regional product centre where local wines, Côtes de Meuse and Côtes de Toul, and foods can be tasted and bought.

Old mint. Hôtel de la Monnaie at Vic-sur-Seille (WZ) in an old Carmelite convent where Lorraine coins were minted from 1383–1625. Fee.

World War I battlefields. Various tours are possible between Éparges, a hamlet in the north of WZ, and Verdun to see the forts of Tavannes, Vaux, Douaumont, etc. Ask tourist offices for details.

Fêtes/fairs. Every village has its annual *jour de fête*. Some are unusual: *escargots* at Thiaucourt on 1 July; mushrooms at Jaulny on 5 Aug.; wines at St-Maurice-sous-les-Côtes on 24 June.

WHERE TO STAY

There are a wide variety of campsites at Sommedieue, Bonzée, Étang de Madine, Jaulny, Thiaucourt and Réchicourt-le-Château. Youth hostels are in St-Mihiel, Nancy, Metz and Villers-lès-Nancy. Alternatives are *gîtes ruraux, chambres d'hôte* and *camping à la ferme*. There are *auberges* and hotels in all the towns surrounding the park, but try the smaller places such as Chambley, Thiaucourt, St-Mihiel, Dieuze, Mittersheim and Château-Salins inside the park.

TOURIST OFFICES

Pont-à-Mousson. 52 pl. Duroc (☎ 83.81.06.90).
Toul. Parvis de la Cathédrale (☎ 83.64.11.69).
St-Mihiel. Pavillon Centre Ville (☎ 29.89.04.50).

REGIONAL VISITS

Nancy. The old town, Place Stanislaus, Place de la Carrière, ducal palace, museums of history and *beaux-arts*, zoological gardens and tropical aquarium.

Metz. Cathédrale St-Étienne, 4thC Église St-Pierre-aux-Nonnains, Porte des Allemands, museum of art and history, riverside walks.

Verdun. Cathedral and cloisters, episcopal palace and *ville haute*.

Toul. Cathédrale St-Étienne, Église St-Gengoult and cloisters, municipal museum.

VOSGES DU NORD

Region: ALSACE-LORRAINE

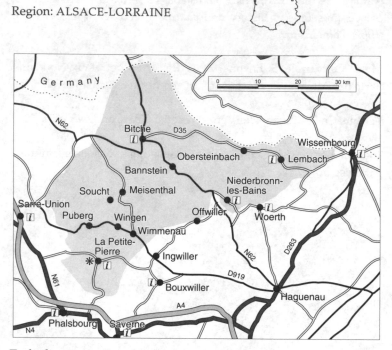

Tucked away in France's northeast corner between the plain of the Rhine and the Lorraine plateau is the Parc Naturel Régional des Vosges du Nord. The park is distinctive because its 120,000 ha have been awarded UNESCO's title of 'Biosphere Reserve' as part of the international 'Man and the Biosphere' programme. It is also remarkable because it contains 40 *châteaux-forts* and 15 museums and has a chunk of the Maginot Line running through it! Part of its northern boundary is linked to the German nature park of Palatinat/Pfälzerwald, and the Lorraine nature park is 30 km west. In the triangle Bitche–Saverne–Wissembourg are 94 communes with a population of 85,000. Although the park is at the north end of the Vosges massif, the average height is only 500 m and half the area is covered with dense forest where game flourish and lakes, moors, peat bogs and sandy grasslands produce interesting flora. Man has lived and fought here for thousands of years and megalithic monuments and Roman remains are proof. Traditional industries continue, such as crystal manufacture and wood-working.

Twenty farmers within the park offer delicious local products, and Wissembourg produces famous brands of sparkling wines. Local folklore *spectacles* and *fêtes* take place in every pretty half-timbered village during high summer. The Park HQ has the best literature of any of the French regions with comprehensive information on fauna, flora, museums and walks. Communications within the park are good, with the N62 Haguenau–Bitche and D919 Haguenau–Sarre-Union running west–east through it.

Maps. Michelin 57, 957; IGN 12.

Access. From Strasbourg northwest by A4, exit Saverne. From Nancy east by N74 and D955/N4 to Phalsbourg. From Metz east by A4 to Sarre-Union. SNCF stations at Strasbourg, Colmar, Mulhouse and Metz with connections to Haguenau, Wissembourg and Bitche. Local buses are frequent from Haguenau, Wissembourg and Bitche.

Park HQ. Maison du Parc-Château, 67290 La Petite-Pierre (☎ 88.70.46.55). A very modern Park HQ is situated within a handsome 12thC château behind the local church of the fortified village, reached by the D178/D122 from Saverne or the D7 from Bouxwiller.

FAUNA

Wild boar, stag, red deer, roe deer, red squirrel and wild cat abound; the Park HQ has produced illustrated leaflets on the stone marten (*fouine*), marten (*martre*) and barn owl (*chouette effraie*). Many species can be seen in the animal park of Schwartzbach 2 km east of La Petite-Pierre. 130 bird species have been noted including 84 nesting birds such as capercaillie, peregrine falcon and Tengmalm owl. The 18 ha Étang de Baerenthal is reached by the N62 to Bannstein and a marked forest trail takes you south to the lake where there is parking and an observation post. Some of the 27 bird species which can be seen here are osprey, grey heron, tufted duck, teal, coot, crested grebe and kingfisher. Apr.–May in the morning is the best time to watch the migrants returning, and in the woods you can hear the cuckoo. The rivers Mittelbach, Rothbach and Schwartzbach, and the Imstall, Fosse, Hanau and Hassellfurt Étangs, contain a wide range of freshwater fish.

FLORA AND VEGETATION

Over 600 species have been recorded in the park. The Forêt de Mouterhouse has for instance oak, beech and Scots pine, and among the conifers are three varieties of fir. The landscape consists of three different types: the Lorraine plateau in the west, a hilly, rocky region in the centre and the Piedmont Vosges hills in the east. Many fossils have been found in the limestone rocks. Woodlands account for 60 per cent of the area and the rest consists of grazed grassland, hay meadows, copses and peat bogs on sandy soils at higher altitudes. The red cliffs and soil are a feature. In the valley of Schwartzbach near Neunhoffen is a large bog with marshland flora: wood grapefern, water arum, roundleaf sundew and pink alpine laurel. The park's leaflet *Sentiers Forestiers* has trails around Geyerstein, Herrenberg, Neuwalk, Scherhol, Soultzerkopf and Staerbelswald. The Étang de Hanau north of Bannstein off the N62 is perhaps the best botanical site in the park with seven observation points from which to watch birds and insects and to identify the marshland flora. These include Traunstein orchids, *marais myrtille* and carniverous plants. The botanical gardens in Saverne have many rare local species.

WHAT TO DO

Walks. The Grande Randonnée 53 crosses the park between Saverne, La Petite-Pierre, Wimmenau, Lichtenberg, Niederbronn, Obersteinbach, Climbach and Wissembourg. The GR 532 starts at Phalsbourg, goes north to La Petite-Pierre and Wingen and then runs through the Forêt d'Ingwiller, Baerenthal and Sturzelbronn. The GR 531 starts west of Wissembourg near Château de Fleckenstein, then goes south through Niederbronn-les-Bains, Ingwiller, Saverne and Dabo. The Park HQ has suggestions for 'theme' walks – forestry, birdlife, history, archaeology and architecture. For instance there is the 6 km Sentier Géologique de Bastberg near Bouxwiller to explore where 50-million-year-old fossils have been found. Another covers part of the Maginot Line between Lembach, Dombach-Neunhoffen and Woerth.

Horse-riding. The Park HQ has a list of *centres équestres* including Saverne, Bitche, Sarre-Union and Puberg.

Cycling/VTT. Apart from SNCF stations at Strasbourg, Colmar and Mulhouse the tourist offices at Cerney (☎ 89.75.50.35) and St-Marie-aux-Mines (☎ 89.58.80.50) rent cycles by the day or week. Park HQ will suggest VTT trails.

Canoe/kayak. Saverne has a *port de plaisance* and Woerth has two centres at 9 Grand Rue and 15 rue de Genève (☎ 88.35.27.20) where canoes and kayaks can be hired.

Other activities. Delta-planing, hang-gliding, fishing and three aero-clubs – ask Park HQ for details.

WHAT TO SEE

Châteaux. It is invidious to make a choice among the 40 in the park. Try to see the Citadelle de Bitche, Apr.–Nov. (☎ 87.96.18.82); Château de Fleckenstein near Lembach, Mar.–Nov. (☎ 88.70.46.55); and Forteresse de Lichtenberg, Apr.–Oct. (☎ 88.89.98.72).

Museums. These are in Bouxwiller (history of Hanau region) (☎ 88.70.70.16); Meisenthal (glass, crystal) (☎ 87.96.91.51); Merkwiller-Pechelbronn (Maison du Pétrole) (☎ 88.80.77.85); Offwiller (folklore, arts) (☎ 88.89.30.98); Niederbronn (archaeology) (☎ 88.80.36.37); La Petite-Pierre (folklore, arts) (☎ 88.70.48.65); Pfaffenhoffen (Alsatian paintings, folklore) (☎ 88.07.70.23); Phalsbourg (military history) (☎ 87.24.12.26); Sarre-Union (heraldry) (☎ 88.00.28.08); Soucht (clog-making) (☎ 87.96.91.52); Obersteinbach (*châteaux-forts*) (☎ 88.09.55.47); Eschwiller (working mill, waterwheel) (☎ 87.96.72.18); Woerth (Franco-Prussian War) (☎ 88.09.30.21); Saverne (art, history, archaeology) (☎ 88.91.06.28); Wissembourg/Westercamp (folklore, military history, arts, archaeology) (☎ 88.54.28.14); Bitche, in the citadel (arms, military history) (☎ 87.96.18.82).

Maginot Line. Musée National de la Fortification at Bitche/Simserhof (☎ 87.96.14.55) Mar.–Dec. exc. Mon. Ouvrage du Four à Chaux at Lembach (☎ 88.94.43.16). Easter–mid-Nov.

Churches. Neuwiller-lès-Saverne (12thC abbey); Marmoutier (abbey);

Weiterswiller; Saverne (cloisters); Sarre-Union (several); and Wissembourg (13thC St-Pierre-et-Paul) are worth a look.

Spa towns. Niederbronn-les-Bains off the N62 northwest of Haguenau
is the best known with thermal baths, casino, park and good hotels.
Merkwiller-Pechelbronn in the Seltzbach valley is another smaller spa
town.

Picturesque villages. Some are enchanting and most photogenic such
as Bouxwiller, Cléebourg, Lembach, Niedersteinbach, Oberbronn-
Zinnswiller and Obersteinbach.

Crafts. Practically every village has one or more crafts to offer including Soufflenheim, Mothern, Sarreguemines and St-Louis-lès-Bitche.
The Maison du Parc has a list of 20 farmers who offer cheeses, honey,
foie gras and other delicacies.

WHERE TO STAY

Within the park there are youth hostels, many *gîtes* and *gîtes d'étape*
(Climbach, Oberbronn). Ask at Park HQ or tourist offices for a list.
There are campsites at Bitche, Baerenthal, Saverne, Oberbronn and
Étang de Hanau. *Auberges* and small hotels are in Bitche, La Petite-
Pierre, Wissembourg, Niederbronn-les-Bains and Bouxwiller.

TOURIST OFFICES

Bitche (☎ 87.96.00.13). Bouxwiller (☎ 88.89.47.20). Lembach
(☎ 88.94.43.81). Niederbronn-les-Bains (☎ 88.09.17.00). La Petite-Pierre
(☎ 88.70.44.30). Phalsbourg (☎ 87.24.12.26). Sarre-Union (☎ 88.00.18.40).
Saverne (☎ 88.91.80.47). Wissembourg (☎ 88.94.14.55). Woerth (☎
88.09.30.21).

REGIONAL VISITS

West to the nature park of Lorraine and further afield to the cities of
Colmar, Mulhouse and Strasbourg.

FORÊT D'ORIENT

Region: CHAMPAGNE

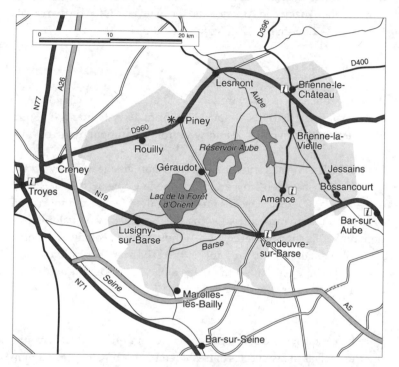

This park was created in 1970 and consists of 60,200 ha located to the east of Troyes, the historic capital of the Champagne region, famous since the Middle Ages for its trade fairs, churches, stained-glass manufacture and museums. The region is called 'Champagne Humide', as the landscape mingles great lakes and forests, valley pastures and low wooded hills. The park is in the *département* of Aube, is composed of 47 communes and has a population of 90,000. Among the main features are two large lakes; one of 2600 ha is a reservoir of the river Aube, and the other, 300 ha smaller, a reservoir of the river Seine. In between is the ornithological reserve, covering 300 ha, to which access is forbidden in order to protect the wildlife. The lake is important as a feeding- and resting-place for migratory and overwintering wildfowl. The forests

29

account for 16,000 ha and take their name, Forêt d'Orient, from the 13thC owners – les Chevaliers d'Orient, Templiers et Hospitaliers. The park is bounded on the north by Creney, Piney, Lesmont and Brienne-le-Château and on the south by Lusigny-sur-Barse, Vendeuvre-sur-Barse and Bossancourt. Rivers in or near the park include the Seine, Barse, Aube, Auzon and Amance and the main lake is fed by two canals to and from the Seine, near Lusigny-sur-Barse.

Maps. Michelin 61; IGN 22.

Access. From Troyes eastwards by D960 or N19. From Châlons-sur-Marne southwards by N77 and D396 from Vitry-le-François. From St-Dizier southwest on D400 and west from Chaumont by A5 or N19.

Park HQ. The Maison du Parc is in the small village of Piney on the D960 halfway between Troyes and Brienne-le-Château (☎ 25.41.35.57), 0900–1200, 1400–1800. The old farmhouse doubles as an information centre and nature museum, showing the local history of water irrigation, timber floating, mineralogy, ornithology and geology. Free entry. There is a small Maison du Parc on the D79 near the ornithological reserve. The open-air museum village of Ste-Marie-du-Lac, with half-timbered buildings, should be seen.

FAUNA

Wild boar, stags, roe deer, red deer, red fox and red squirrels can be seen, as well as many species of freshwater fish – bream, carp, salmon and trout – but the park is mainly known for its 23 bird species. These include the white-tailed eagle, crane, merganser, harrier, buzzard, grey heron, goose, shrike, woodpecker, treecreeper, grebe and duck. Over 1000 bean geese winter on the lake and occasionally rare birds, such as the sea eagle, can be seen. The total wildfowl count is about 6000 birds, including the unusual scaup, smew, goosander and shelduck.

FLORA AND VEGETATION

The forested massif woodland is dominated by oaks, but tucked away among ferns and ivy are 300 species of mushroom. Around the 300 lakes and ponds are alder, willow and poplar, as well as rushes and reeds in the surrounding wet meadows. The soil is mainly clay, which retains water and is useful to local makers of pottery. When the Aube reservoir is finished, the benefit to the flora and fauna will be considerable.

WHAT TO DO

Walks. The Grande Randonnée 24 enters the park from the south at Marolles-lès-Bailly and Villeneuve-au-Chêne and crosses through the main forest east of the lake to Amance, where it splits to go east towards Bar-sur-Aube and, as the 24B, north to Brienne-le-Château and Lesmont, and northeast towards the large Lac de Der-Chantecoq. The GR 24A runs parallel to the park but a few km south, through Bar-sur-Seine to Noé-les-Mallets, where it joins the GR 24. There are many local walks through woodland by the lakeside.

Fishing. There are anglers' societies (a permit is needed to fish) at Lusigny-sur-Barse, Jessains and Bossancourt.

Horse-riding. *Centres équestres* are at Le Menilot, Radonvilliers, Brienne-la-Vieille and Vendeuvre-sur-Barse.

Sailing. *Sports nautiques* from Géraudot and Mesnil-St-Père beside the Lac de la Forêt d'Orient.

Canoe/kayak. Rentals from the 'port' on the east side of Lac de la Forêt d'Orient.

Cycling/VTT. Rental from Park HQ.

Bathing. Fine sandy beaches are on the lake at Géraudot and Mesnil-St-Père.

WHAT TO SEE

Museums. *Ecomusée* in Brienne-la-Vieille; Musée Napoléon in Brienne-le-Château, 1000–1200, 1400–1800 (closed Tue.): the Emperor studied military history there. In Troyes, museums of Modern Art, Beaux-Arts, Bonneterie, History and Folklore.

Ornithological reserve. North of Lac de la Forêt d'Orient, best seen from the D79.

Wildlife reserve. Forêt de Piney on the east side of Lac de la Forêt d'Orient has 80 ha with captive wild animals – boar, deer, etc.

Châteaux. Brienne, Vendeuvre-sur-Barse, Bratigny (Piney) and Juvanzé.

Churches. Interesting churches are at Vendeuvre-sur-Barse, Mesnil-St-Père, Géraudot, Thennelières, Laubressel, Rouilly, Piney, Brienne-le-Château, Vauchonvilliers, Puits-et-Nuisement. There is an old abbey at Montreuil-sur-Barse.

Wine-tasting/buying. Champagne and local table wines can be tasted/bought at Trannes on the D396 halfway between Bar-sur-Aube and Brienne-le-Château.

Roman road. The old road in the north of the park between Brienne-la-Vieille and Brienne-le-Château has been restored. The legions once marched along it from Milan to Boulogne.

Son et lumière. Throughout the summer at the Château de Vendeuvre.

Hydraulic dam (*barrage*). Guided visits. Details from Park HQ.

Craft visits. Amance and Brienne-la-Vieille have a number of *poteries* (potters) and *tuileries* (tile-makers).

Ornithological visits/studies. Maison du Parc has the summer programme.

WHERE TO STAY

Youth hostel at Mesnil-St-Père and *gîtes d'étape* for walkers at La Loge-aux-Chèvres and Amance. There are *gîtes* (bed and breakfast) at Bossancourt, Géraudot, Lusigny-sur-Barse, Magny-Fouchard, Pel-et-Der and Vauchonvilliers. There are several campsites at Mesnil-St-Pierre and others at Brienne-la-Vieille and Géraudot. Small *auberges* are to be found in most of the villages around the park. There are many hotels in Troyes and others in Brienne-le-Château and Bar-sur-Aube.

TOURIST OFFICES

The main offices are in Troyes (pop. 65,000), 16 bd Carnot (☎ 25.73.00.36) and 24 quai Dampierre (☎ 25.73.36.88).

Bar-sur-Aube. Mairie (☎ 25.27.04.21).

Also minor SIs at Vendeuvre-sur-Barse (☎ 25.41.33.09), Amance (☎ 25.41.34.08), Brienne-le-Château (☎ 25.77.80.31).

REGIONAL VISIT

Thirty kilometres northeast by D400/D384 is the large Lac de Der-Chantecoq, another ornithological reserve for migrant birds, particularly of European cranes. Short guided boat tours leave from Giffaumont. Tourist office (☎ 26.41.62.80).

BALLONS DES VOSGES

Region: ALSACE-LORRAINE

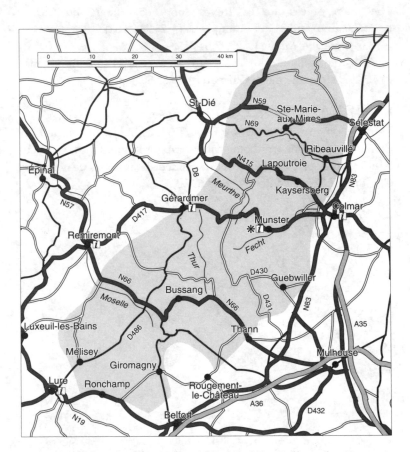

Created in 1989, the Parc Naturel Régional des Ballons des Vosges is one of three such parks in the northeast corner of France. Almost on the frontier with Germany, it was the scene of many grim battles in World Wars I and II. A large park of 300,000 ha, with 200 communes containing a population of 223,000, it is spread over no fewer than four *départements* – Vosges, Haut-Rhin, Haute-Saône and Territorie de Belfort. Locally it is called *Ligne Bleue des Vosges* because 55 per cent of its area is forested with fir trees and beech. Nearly 600 people are employed in woodworking and forestry activities. The *Ballons* are a line of old volcanic craters of between 1100 and 1424 m in depth. The Route des Crêtes, which starts at Thann, continues through the Grand Ballon near Guebwiller and then by means of the magic roads D431 and D430 winds north towards the D61 which begins at the Col de la Schlucht. The many ranges of hills, some of them containing ski resorts, contrast sharply with the fertile valleys along which run the rivers Chajoux, Petite Meurthe, Meurthe, Fecht, Strengbach, Ill, Lauch, Thur and others which eventually flow into the Rhine. In the valleys are the prosperous little towns of Remiremont (pop. 10,900), Gérardmer (pop. 9800), Thann (pop. 7800), Munster (pop. 4700) and Ribeauville (pop. 4600). In the heart of this lovely park it is difficult to realise that it is bordered by five large towns – Colmar to the east, Mulhouse and Belfort to the southeast, Épinal to the west and St-Dié to the northwest. There is a network of good roads within the park including the D417 Colmar–Munster–Gérardmer in a west–east direction and the N415 from Colmar–Kayserberg–Lapoutroie *en route* to St-Dié. Just west of Colmar is one of the most famous wine routes in the world, where the *vins d'Alsace* are grown. The wine villages of Riquewihr, Turckheim and a dozen others are quite beautiful but crammed full of tourists in midsummer. And of course the Alsatian cuisine ranks among the best in France. But the foremost reason for visiting this 'new' park is to see its extensive fauna and flora, preferably on foot, since no fewer than seven Grandes Randonnées traverse the area.

Nature reserves. For conservation of the rich flora and fauna a number of protected reserves have been created: La Tourbière (peat bog) de Machais (145 ha), Les Hautes-Chaumes du Tanet-Gazon de Faing and the forests on the massif of Ventron (1500 ha). And more recently the Lac de Retournemer, the glacial cirques of Frankenthal (Stosswihr) and Missheimle, and the Ballon de Servance (Haute-Saône).

Maps. Michelin 62, 66, 87; IGN 31.

Access. From Colmar westwards by D417 and N415. From Sélestat to St-Dié by N59. South from St-Dié by N415 and D8. From Mulhouse northwest to Thann, Bussang and Remiremont by N66. SNCF trains leave Colmar for Munster and Gérardmer and from St-Dié go to

Sélestat. There are frequent bus services through the park, usually west–east and vice versa.

Park HQ. In a handsome manor house at 1 rue de l'Église, 68140 Munster (☎ 89.77.29.04). Munster is 20 km west of Colmar on the D417. There is a wide range of activities on offer including unusual ones such as Montgolfier ballooning and delta-planing as well as skiing and visiting World War I battlefields.

FAUNA

Wild boar, red deer, roe deer, pine marten and red squirrel are quite often seen. Recently lynx have been reintroduced – the only wild ones in France. Many chamois can be noted and a visit to the Parc Animalier, Fougerolles-St-Valbert (Easter–Sept.) off the N57 in the southwest corner of the park is recommended. Sheep transhumance takes place each spring between valley and hillside pastures. Birdlife is extensive. Capercaillie (*grand tétras*), peregrine falcons, Tengmalm owls, breasted blackbirds, great tit, cuckoos, occasional storks, egrets, wild duck and geese can be seen and, around the hundreds of lakes and ponds, dozens of nesting species, as the park is on a migratory passage. Munster has introduced a stork park. A wide range of fish species are found including crayfish, trout, burbot, eel, water salamander (*triton*) and bream. Butterflies and dragonflies flit among the alpine flora. CIN (Centre Initiation à la Nature) (☎ 89.82.23.70), on the Route des Crêtes on the D430 south of Col de la Schlucht, near Wildenstein, arranges a variety of practical fauna/flora walks.

FLORA AND VEGETATION

Firs, pines, spruce, mountain elm, maple, yew, ash and beech cover most hillsides apart from escarpments such as the Hautes Chaumes, which have a wide range of alpine vegetation such as gentians, anemones, orchids, alpine lettuce and arnica. One species worth looking for is *aconit-tue-loup* (wolves disappeared long ago!). Peat bogs (*tourbières*), marshes and wetlands (*marais*) cover considerable areas protecting birdlife and wild flowers such as Siberian iris, swordflag (*glaieul*) and wild rose. Look for wood geraniums, bilberries, blueberries, cranberries, sundew and a range of medicinal herbs such as purple digitalis. The major forests are Luxeuil, Remspach and Vosges. The Club Vosgien has a daily programme in July–Sept. of fauna/flora expeditions. The three branches are Cie des Accompagnateurs at Munster; Vosges en Marche, Basse-sur-le-Rupt; and Vosges Evasion, Gérardmer. Details from Park HQ.

Ballons. Among the better-known craters are the Grand Ballon, Petit Ballon, Ballon de Servance and Ballon d'Alsace.

Lakes. Southwest of the main Vosges massif in the southwest corner of the park is the Plateau des Mille Étangs, an area between Luxeuil-les-Bains, Lure and Le Tillot, although the figure of 1000 is perhaps Gallic hyperbole! Larger lakes are to be found further north near Gérardmer, along the Thur valley and Lac Blanc near Ste-Marie-aux-Mines, Gunsbach, Neuweiher and Sondernach. Local spa water is bottled commercially at Soultzbach-les-Bains.

ECOMUSÉES

Ungersheim near Ensisheim (☎ 89.48.23.44).

Ecomusée de Haute-Alsace, Pulversheim (N83/D430) just outside the southeast corner of the park on the way to Mulhouse. It has a mill, gardens, fortified château and working craftspeople in 18thC houses.

WHAT TO DO

Walks. The Club Vosgien has marked out 6000 km of walks inside the park, more than any other French nature park, and seven Grandes Randonnées range through it. The GR 5 arrives at Sélestat in the northeast corner, runs west to Ste-Marie-aux-Mines, then southwest to follow the Route des Crêtes to Thann, goes west to Ballon d'Alsace and doubles back east to Masevaux and south towards Belfort. The GR 7 arrives at Remiremont on the western boundary and travels southeast to the Ballon de Servance via Château-Lambert. The GR 53 comes in from the northwest at Col de Donon and spawns the 531, 532 and 533, which run south through the park. The GR 59 starts at Ballon de Servance, heads southwest to Bettany and Ronchamp, then disappears southeast to Montbeliard. The Club Vosgien recommends five circular walks from Soultzeren or Munster ranging from 1½ to 5½ hours.

Horse-riding. There are two dozen *centres équestres* within the park and hundreds of km of bridleways. Details from Park HQ.

VTT. This is now a major sport on mountain bikes which can be rented in many places including five in or near Munster. The Championnat de France de VTT over 18 or 35 km takes place near Munster in mid-Sept.

Canoe/kayak. There are many opportunities including at Villersexel (☎ 84.20.30.87).

Caving (*spéléologie*). For practical courses ☎ 84.28.08.85 or enquire at tourist offices.

Fishing. Plenty of availability but a permit is needed. Ask at tourist offices.

Rock climbing. Details can be obtained from Association Munster Escalade (☎ 89.23.49.76 or 84.28.08.85).

Horse-drawn caravans. *Promenades en calèche* from six *centres équestres* at Metzeral, Luttenbach, Gunsbach (two), Wasserbourg and Munster.

Montgolfier ballooning. Reservations can be made through Aerovision (☎ 89.77.22.81) or Becker (☎ 84.22.08.17).

Skiing. The main *ski nordique* and *ski alpine* stations are at Gérardmer, La Bresse, Mulbach-sur-Munster, Markstein, Ballon d'Alsace and Lac Blanc (Le Bonhomme), all at heights about 1250 m. Advice from Office de Tourisme, Munster (☎ 89.71.31.80).

Cheese farm visits. The Route du Fromage visits up to 25 *fermes-auberges* where you can stay and sample local cuisine including Munster cheeses. Ask tourist offices for a map.

Fêtes/fairs. Every town and village has a summer *fête*, often connected with the local wine, food or industrial activity (*fête montagnarde*, *fête folklorique* or *fête campagnarde*). Ask for dates from tourist offices.

WHAT TO SEE

Museums

Musée Schweitzer/African Art, 8 rue de Munster, Gunsbach (☎ 89.77.31.42).

Musée Schlitte/Métiers du Bois, 56 rue Principale, Muhlbach/Munster (☎ 89.77.61.07).

Vestiges 1914–18, World War I battle Musée du Linge, Müller-Stosswihr (☎ 89.71.23.54) at Ampfersbach where 20,000 soldiers died.

Musée des Amis de Thann and art/folklore museum at Thann.

Musée de la Forge (Sun. only), Etueffont (☎ 84.54.60.40).

Musée Albert-Demard (closed Tue.), Château-Lambert (☎ 84.20.43.09).

Musées de la Mine (Easter–Oct.), Giromagny and Ronchamp.

Churches. Notre-Dame-du-Haut near Ronchamp; Murbach; Thann; Abbaye St-Colomban at Luxeuil-les-Bains; Abbaye de Lure; 11thC Romanesque church at Mélisey; Abbaye Mont-de-Vannes at Fresse.

Silver mines. Visit the 16thC silver mines of Val d'Argent near Ste-Marie-aux-Mines on the N69 halfway between Sélestat and St-Dié. Also the mines and galleries at Giromagny.

Châteaux are to be seen at Thann, Rougemont-le-Château, Giromagny (northeast) and seven in a line on the eastern boundary of the park between Ribeauvillé and northwest of Eguisheim. Château-Kintzheim has a wild eagle sanctuary, and the finest is that of Haut-Koenigsbourg with its triple defensive ramparts and keep.

Botanical garden. Haut-Chitelet, Col de la Schlucht, open June–Oct. Fee.

Food crafts. Taste cheese, honey, *foie gras*, fruit, smoked meats, etc., at Maison des Vosges (Zim), pl. du Vieux-Gérardmer, Gérardmer.

WHERE TO STAY

There is a huge range of *gîtes ruraux*, *chalet-refuges*, *fermes-auberges*, campsites and *centres de vacance* inside the park. Hotels and *auberges* are located in every town (100 in the Munster valley). Ask for details from tourist offices.

TOURIST OFFICES

Gérardmer. Maison des Vosges, pl. du Vieux-Gérardmer (☎ 29.60.08.75).
Rothenbach. Centre Initiation à la Nature, rte des Crêtes.
Munster. Pl. du Marché (☎ 89.77.31.80).
Lure. 35 rue Carnot (☎ 84.62.80.52).
Remiremont (☎ 29.62.23.70).
Colmar (☎ 89.41.02.29).

REGIONAL VISITS

Strasbourg with cathedral, Rohan château, museums, covered bridges, old town, *la Petite France*, canal promenades and parliament building.
Colmar has its old town, bridges, museums and *la Petite Venise*.
Belfort with château, planetarium and tropical aquarium.
Mulhouse with four museums, zoological gardens, churches and Hôtel de Ville.
Alsace Wine Route. Approximately 30 km north–south on or off the N83/D10 west of Colmar, including the wine villages of Riquewihr, Ribeauville and Turckheim.

MORVAN

Region: BURGUNDY

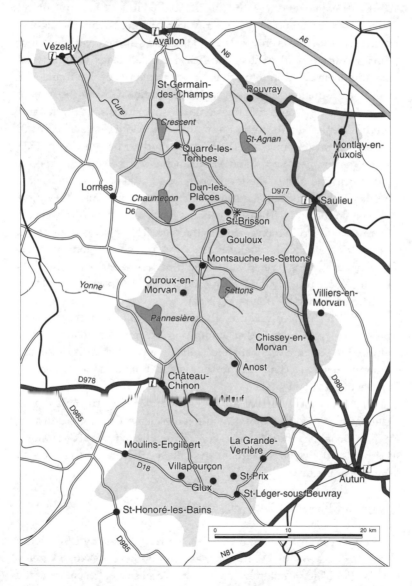

This superb Burgundian nature park was founded in 1970 and covers 175,000 ha – half forest, half pasturelands. Although parts of it are in the *départements* of Saône-et-Loire, Côte-d'Or and Yonne, 50 per cent is in Nièvre. There are 64 communes but only 33,000 inhabitants. It is south of Avallon and west of Autun and it includes Château-Chinon on the western boundary. It is mainly a granite massif, but the highest point at Haut-Folin is only 900 m and the peaks often stay under snow during autumn and winter. The heavy rainfall leads to numerous streams which feed into the rivers and tributaries of the Yonne and Cure. There are five huge lakes within the park – Crescent, St-Agnan, Settons, Chaumeçon and Pannesière. The main forests are St-Prix and Breuil-Chenus, and the loftiest mountains are Mont Genièvre (637 m), Mont Beuvray (821 m), Haut Folin (901 m) and Roches-de-Glenne (559 m) in the southern sector and Montsauche (650 m) and Chaumeçon (598 m) in the north. The local towns are Saulieu on the northeast border, Château-Chinon, Montsauche-les-Settons and beautiful Vézelay in the north. The Celts called a Black Mountain *Mor-Van* and there are still Druid monuments in the park. The *oppidum* of Bibracte, capital of the Gaulish tribe of Edens, was located on Mont Beuvray. Vercingetorix, king of the Gauls, fought battles here against Caesar's legions. More recently the French Maquis used the park as a centre of resistance against the occupying Nazis.

In the lush green pastures Burgundian cattle and sheep graze peacefully, particularly the ubiquitous creamy Charolais. Roads within the park are well kept and well signed, and there is lots to see – nature reserves, châteaux, museums and Romanesque churches – and activities of all kinds.

The Morvan is famous for its cuisine: venison, river fish, goat cheeses and modest wines grown near Vézelay (the best are further east in Dijon–Beaune–Mâcon). There is a small spa town at St-Honoré-les-Bains, where you can recover and take the thermal waters and also gamble at the casino.

Maps. Michelin 69; IGN 36, 306.

Access. From Autun west by M78. From Nevers east by D978. From Saulieu southwest by D977. From Auxerre southeast by N6 to Vézelay or Avallon. The A6 autoroute passes north and east of the park and the best stopping-off point is east of Avallon. The SNCF TGV service goes to Autun, Nevers, Clamecy and Avallon and there is a minor service to Château-Chinon. Many bus services cross through the park, and Avallon and Autun have small airports.

Park HQ. Maison du Parc, St-Brisson, 58230 Montsauche (☎ 86.78.70.16). It is situated in a large rambling château on the D6 off the D977 14 km west of Saulieu between dolmens and a deer park. Each of the tourist offices mentioned later has information about the park, activities and lodgings.

FAUNA

There are wild boar (*sangliers*), fox and squirrels in the woods. Roe deer (*chevreuils*), red deer and wild boar have a nature reserve in the Anost forest east of Château-Chinon off the D2. Roe deer have a reserve in the Forêt de Breuil-Chenue close to the Park HQ, and for fallow deer there is a reserve, La Vernuie, in the Forêt au Duc near to Quarré-les-Tombes on the D10 northwest of Saulieu. A wide range of birds including some migrants is to be found in the large lakes with duck, geese and herons. They feed on trout, tench, perch, pike, roach and many other fish species. Reptiles abound with grass- and some venomous snakes, so take care in the spring breeding season.

FLORA AND VEGETATION

The Morvan massif is covered by 90,000 ha of woodland mainly planted with copper beech, hornbeam, oak, silver birch and conifers. The wild flowers are superb – a full range of orchids, angelica, purple digitalis, marsh trefoil, *la reine des prés*, broom, rushes, *l'impatience-ne-me-touchez-pas*, *la grande luzule* and many others. The new botanical garden, the 'Herbularium', has 160 Morvan species divided into 32 sections. It is located outside the Park HQ, which organises courses in the study of medicinal plants and herbs. At Uchon in the southeast look for the unique *flore lacutres*.

WHAT TO DO

Walks. There are hundreds of km of signed walks in the park and the Park HQ has devised a 220 km *Grands Lacs* circuit divided into ten *étapes* called the *Tour du Morvan*. Also the GR 13 winds through the park

43

with its derivations, e.g. GR 131. It starts in the south from Bourbon-Lancy, then runs between Toulon-sur-Arroux and Luzy, goes over Mont Dône and Mont Beuvray, then through the Forêts de St-Prix and d'Anost, past the *enclos des sangliers* alongside the river Cure and the Lac des Settons, the Park HQ and St-Agnan, and northwards past Abbaye de la Pierre-qui-Vire (Balancing Rock) towards Avallon and Vézelay on its way to Auxerre.

Horse-riding. There are 17 *centres équestres* including Château-Chinon, Dun-les-Places, Montsauche, Montlay-en-Auxois, Ouroux-en-Morvan, Rouvray, St-Germain-des-Champs, St-Léger-sous-Beuvray, Saulieu, Villapourçon and St-Honoré-les-Bains.

Aquatic centres. For sailing or canoe/kayak there are *ports de plaisance* on the six lakes – Settons, Pannesière, Chamboux, Chaumeçon, St-Agnan and Crescent. In addition one can canoe and kayak on the rivers Cure, Cousin and Chalaux. Details from Association Pleine Nature en Morvan, 58230 Montsauche (☎ 86.76.10.11).

Cycling/VTT. The Maison du Parc has a dozen cycles for hire.

Skiing. There are several small ski resorts at St-Prix/Haut-Folin and Arleuf. Information from Park HQ or Mairie at Glux (☎ 86.78.62.85).

Climbing. There are five *centres escalades* at Dun-les-Places, Pierre Perthuis, Anost, La Grande-Verrière and Montsauche.

WHAT TO SEE

Châteaux. From north to south they are at Lichères-sur-Yonne, Bierre-lès-Semur, St-Andeux, Chastellux-sur-Cure, Bazoches, Saulieu, Villemolin, Cervon, St-Martin-de-la-Mer, Villiers-en-Morvan, Menessaire, Chissey-en-Morvan, Châtillon-en-Bazois, St-Léger-de-Fougeret, Moulins-Engilbert, La Grande-Verrière, Monthelon, Vandenesse, Larochemillay and Monjeu. Check with the tourist offices on opening times and entry fees.

Museums. At Avallon is the Musée de l'Avallonnais (archaeology, prehistory). Autun has four museums – Rolin (prehistory, architecture),

Lapidaire, Cathédrale (sacred art) and Natural History. At Château-Chinon is a museum of folklore, costume and arts. St-Père-de-Vézelay has an archaeological museum. Near the Park HQ at St-Brisson is an evocative museum dedicated to the World War II resistance movement, which was helped by British agents. St-Léger-sous-Beuvray has an archaeological museum and there are museums at Arnay-le-Duc and Saulieu (François Pompon animal sculptures). St-Léger-Vauban has a small museum about Marshal Vauban's life and career (July–Sept. p.m.). Check with the tourist offices for opening times, fees, etc.

Churches. Supreme in Burgundy is the majestic Basilique Ste-Madeleine at Vézelay, where St Bernard preached the Second Crusade and Thomas à Becket took refuge and excommunicated King Henry II. Saulieu has its elegant 12thC basilica, St-Androche. Autun has the handsome Romanesque-Gothic cathedral of St-Lazare with 12thC tympan and chaptals. There are 30 other churches, many Romanesque, which are worth visiting, including l'Abbaye de la Pierre-qui-Vire and Avallon's 12thC collegiate Église St-Lazare.

Archaeology. Autun (originally Augustodunum) has the magnificent Roman temple of Janus, amphitheatre, Roman *portes* and ramparts. Many of the Gaulish finds around Mont Beuvray can be seen in the Morvan's archaeological museums at Autun, Avallon, St-Père-de-Vézelay, etc.

Roulottes. Horse-drawn caravans are available for rental from two stables at Lucenay-l'Évêque (☎ 85.82.66.48 and 85.82.69.12) or Vézelay (☎ 86.33.25.77).

Thermal spa. St-Honoré-les-Bains. For information ☎ 86.30.71.70.

Natural sights. The most photogenic are the lakes of Settons and Pannesière, the mountain of Haut-Folin and the waterfalls of Gouloux.

Crafts. Sabot makers at La Grande-Verrière, St-Père-sous-Vézelay, Gouloux; silk weaving at Alligny-en-Morvan; glass working, stone working, pottery, local foods such as cheese, honey, *foie gras* and wine

(Guyard, rue St-Pierre, Vézelay). There is a summer exhibition of craft work beside the Lac des Settons.

WHERE TO STAY

There are over 20 campsites, several youth hostels, a dozen *gîtes d'étape* and many *gîtes ruraux* available. Château-Chinon, Saulieu, Autun, Vézelay, Autun and St-Honoré-les-Bains offer an extensive range of hotels to suit all pockets. Children might like a holiday in the *village de vacances* in the park at St-Agnan.

TOURIST OFFICES

Arnay-le-Duc. 15 rue St-Jacques (☎ 80.90.11.59) (Apr.–Oct.).
Autun. 3 ave. Ch.-de-Gaulle (☎ 85.52.20.34).
Avallon. Pl. de la Collégiale St-Lazare (☎ 86.34.14.19).
Château-Chinon. Rue du Champlin (☎ 86.85.06.58).
Châtillon-en-Bazois. Mairie (☎ 86.84.14.76).
Clamecy. Rue du Grand Marché (☎ 86.27.02.51) (June–Sept.).
Luzy. Mairie (☎ 86.30.02.34).
Saulieu. Maison de Tourisme (N6) (☎ 80.64.00.21).
Vézelay. Rue St-Pierre (☎ 86.33.23.69).

REGIONAL VISITS

Autun. Roman city, cathedral and museums.
Avallon. Ramparts, 15thC clock tower, 12thC church, museums.
Nevers. Ducal palace, convent of Bernadette Soubirous.
Arnay-le-Duc. Motte-Forte, Condé château, 15thC church.
Taizé. Unique monastic ecumenical religious community, Church of the Reconciliation.

HAUT-JURA

Region: FRANCHE-COMTÉ

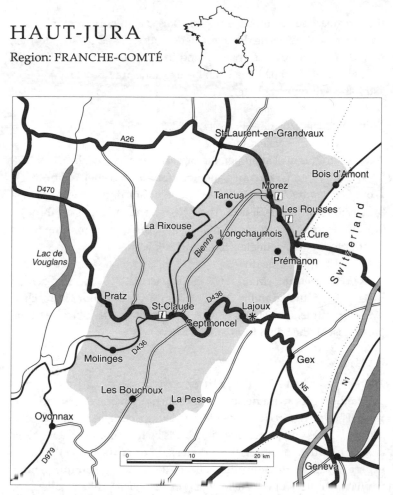

Tucked away in the southeast corner of the *département* of Jura, 40 km northwest of Geneva, lies the Parc Naturel Régional du Haut-Jura. Created in 1986, it covers 62,000 ha with 37 communes and 37,000 inhabitants in the Monts du Jura, an area of limestone plateau hills. These start at 400–900 m and to the east by the Swiss border rise to 1463 m (Mont d'Or) and 1677 m (Mont de la Dôle). Heavily wooded hillsides flank the valleys of the rivers Bienne, Tacon and Lison with many attractive gorges, grottoes, lakes and waterfalls (*cascades*). The only towns of significance are St-Claude and Morez, but there are many charming little villages to explore. There is a major ski resort area in

47

the northeast sector of Les Rousses, Bois d'Armont, Prémanon and Lamoura. The cuisine is distinguished by its smoked meats, Morbier, bleu de Gex and Comté cheeses, and its unusual *vin jaune* (literally, yellow wine) d'Arbois. The main occupations are dairy farming, forestry and salt mining.

Maps. Michelin 70; IGN 37, 38, 44, 3228, 3327/8.

Access. From Lons-le-Saunier, the prefecture town, southeast by N78 to St-Laurent-en-Grandvaux and the northeast corner of the park. From Geneva by N5/D436 to St-Claude. From Bourg-en-Bresse east by D979/D436 to St-Claude. The SNCF from Lyon passes through St-Claude and Morez on its way to Dijon. Buses run from the Swiss frontier town of La Cure to Morez and St-Claude.

Park HQ. Maison du Haut-Jura, Lajoux, 39310 Septmoncel (☎ 84.41.20.37). Situated on the D436 between St-Claude and Gex, reached by a serpentine, mountainous road, it is on the eastern border of the park, close to the Swiss frontier.

FAUNA

There are wild boar, roe deer, red deer, occasional lynx and red squirrel, and in the rivers swim freshwater fish such as bream, carp, tench and trout. The *grand tétras* (capercaillie) is making a comeback. Around the 300 or so lakes and ponds, breeding birds include heron, bittern, egret and many duck including the red-crested pochard. Above the forest expect to see short-toed eagles, and in the woods tree pipits, snipe, whinchats and sedges. There is a *parc zoologique* called Vallée des Rennes at Prémanon.

FLORA AND VEGETATION

Forty per cent of the park's land area is covered by forest. The Forêt du Massacre commemorates the heroism of the World War II resistance. The Forêt de la Joux (2700 ha) is one of the best fir forests in France. Others of note include Avignon, Annuelle, Le Frénois and Risoux. White oak, beech, silver fir, poplar, ash, maple and alder are grown. Conifers grow up to 45 m high and 1.2 m in diameter. Alpine vegetation grows on the slopes including martagon lily, cyclamen and gentian.

48

The word Jura derives from the Latin word for forest and old Roman roads still run through the Forêt de la Joux in the northwest corner, which is managed by the Office National des Forêts. Large peat bogs are sited near La Pesse and Lac de Bellefontaine.

WHAT TO DO

Walks. Several Grandes Randonnées cross the park. The GR 559 arrives in the northeast via Pic de l'Aigle, Morez and Tancua. The GR 5 passes down the French side of the border with Switzerland via Bellefontaine, Bois d'Amont and Les Rousses to Prémanon where the GR 9 links up with it. Altogether there are 900 km of *sentiers balisés*, signed footpaths, in the park.

Skiing. There are 700 km of *pistes balisées*, cross-country ski trails. The resorts of Les Rousses, Bois d'Amont, Prémanon and Lamoura have 200 km of clearly marked *loipes*. The other main resorts are Septmoncel, Les Moussières, Bellefontaine, La Pesse, Longchaumois, Les Molunes, Morez, and Lajoux and Metabief in the far north with 200 km of *loipes*. There are many ski-schools and ski-lifts.

Caving. At Les Bouchoux, around St-Claude. Besain (see p 51). Ask at tourist office.

Canoe/kayak. Rentals at Morez and La Rixouse.

Cycling/VTT. Cycles can be rented at the SNCF stations at Pontarlier, St-Claude and Besançon.

WHAT TO SEE

Pipemaking is still a major craft industry using local woods. Visit St-Lupicin, St-Claude, Leschères, Choux and Chassal. The pipe museum is in St-Claude (☎ 84.45.04.02). June–Sept. 0930–1130, 1400–1830. Fee.

Cheesemaking at Les Bouchoux (*chévrerie du Prieuré*), Bellecombe (*bleu de Gex*), Lamoura (*fromage bleu persillé*), Longchaumois, Les Molunes (*Septmoncel*), Morbier (same name) and Septmoncel (same name).

Diamond museum in St-Claude (☎ 84.45.13.93), mid-June–mid-Sept.

0930–1130. Fee. Exhibition of diamonds, precious gems, cutting techniques. Chassal has a diamond *atelier* (workshop).

Maison de la Boisellerie in Bois d'Amont (☎ 84.60.30.51). History of cooperage and woodworking. June–Sept. Wed., Sat., Sun. p.m. Fee.

Musée de la Lunetterie in Morez (☎ 84.33.08.73). June–Sept. Tue.–Sat. 1400–1800. Fee. The region has been making glasses since the 18thC. Les Rousses is another spectacles-making village.

Maison de la Faune at Prémanon (☎ 84.60.78.50). A natural history museum, it is open all the year. Fee.

Museums. Beaux-Arts in St-Claude and Morez (Jourdain).

Exhibition. Vie et Métiers d'Autrefois. Folklore museum at La Pesse (☎ 84.42.70.48). Wed. p.m. and Sun. Fee.

Grottoes to be seen include Les Bouchoux, Pratz, St-Anne near St-Claude, Célary near Lamoura.

Cascades/fountains at Les Bouchoux (Moulin), Chassal, Pissevieille and Longchaumois.

Churches. The cathedral at St-Claude, St-Lupicin, Molinges and the Roman chapel at Pratz.

Geological site at Cirque de Baume-les-Messieurs.

WHERE TO STAY

Youth hostels and campsites are to be found at Les Rousses, Prémanon, Bellecombe, Vaux-lès-St-Claude and Ravilloles. *Centres d'acceuil* are at Bellefontaine, Les Molunes and in all the ski resorts. Ask at tourist offices for list of *gîtes ruraux*. There are several hotels in St-Claude, Morez and the ski resorts.

TOURIST OFFICES

St-Claude. 1 ave. Belfort (☎ 84.45.34.24)/rue St-Blaise (☎ 84.45.67.57).

Morez. Pl. Jean-Jaurès (☎ 84.33.08.73).
Les Rousses. Station des Rousses (☎ 84.60.02.55).

REGIONAL VISITS

Villars-les-Dombes. Southwest via Nantua, Brou and the N83 to Villars-les-Dombes is a region of lakes famous for its ornithological park and botanical/zoological nature reserve. Of its 23 ha, 9 ha are lakes and 300 species of birds are on display, some caged, but mostly flying free. The reserve is important for migrant species and wintering wildfowl, including black-necked grebe, whiskered tern and little egret. Traditional use of the lakes for fish culture is permitted. An interesting detour northeast of Lyon on the way to the park of Haut-Jura.

Arbois in the north is the Jura wine-growing centre, with a vine-yard/wine museum and the interesting Sarret de Grozon museum containing porcelain and paintings.

Dôle has a medieval centre, Hôtel-Dieu, the abbey of Notre-Dame and several museums.

Besançon has botanical gardens and *beaux-arts*, history and resistance museums.

Salins-les-Bains in the north is a spa centre with 12thC royal baths, noted churches, museums and a casino.

Besain north of the river Aln has 1200 caves in 500 ha – exceptional *spéléologie*.

Poligny has the Franche-Comté cheese museum (☎ 84.37.23.51).

Lons-le-Sauveur is a *ville fleurie* noted for its *muguets* (lilies of the valley), violets and is the HQ of the Fédération de Protection de la Nature du Jura.

VOLCANS D'AUVERGNE

Region: AUVERGNE

The Auvergne is known for its cheeses and music, less so for its nature park founded in 1975, which with an area of 350,000 ha is the largest in France. Situated to the southwest of Clermont-Ferrand in the Cantal and Puy-de-Dôme *départements*, it stretches for 120 km in a north–south direction. One of the key reasons for a visit is to see the dramatic extinct volcano craters – more than a hundred. The park is divided into five regions. In the north the Monts Dôme are a chain of 80 'young' volcanoes of which the Puy de Dôme, 1465 m, is best known and easily reached by the D941 from Clermont-Ferrand. The Sommet du Puy de Dôme is visited by a third of a million people each year mostly in midsummer, which is thus best avoided. In the centre are the Monts Dore with volcanoes 3 million years old dominated by the Puy de Sancy (1886 m) and in the south the Monts du Cantal, the oldest volcanic range, some 20 million years old. The Puy Mary (1785 m) overlooks 12 valleys. The immense pastures of the plateau of Cézallier lie to the centre/east, watered by the rivers Allanche, Alagnon and Couze d'Ardres, which flow into the main river Allier running parallel to the A75. The Signal du Luguet (1551 m) is the highest volcano in this sector. To the west is the old granite plateau of the Artense between the valley of the river Dordogne and the gorges of the Rhue. This area of forests, peat bogs and lakes has exceptional flora and fauna. Although 92,000 people in 130 communes live in this huge park it is still unspoilt. Six Grandes Randonnées cross it for walkers, there are three classified ski resorts and 40 ski centres, castles and Romanesque churches galore. Horse-riding is popular and the rivers provide good canoeing and kayaking. The Auvergne cuisine is well known, with excellent river fish, *petits vins* and the famous Cantal, St-Nectaire and Forme d'Ambert cheeses. After sampling there are ten thermal spas where a rejuvenating cure can be enjoyed!

Maps. Michelin 73, 76; IGN 49, 2432–6, 2531–5.

Access. From Clermont-Ferrand west by D941b or southwest by D941a. From Aurillac northeast by N122. From St-Flour north by D679 or northwest by D926. SNCF to Clermont-Ferrand, Aurillac, St-Flour and locally to St-Nectaire and La Bourboule. A network of roads traverses the park with many local bus services.

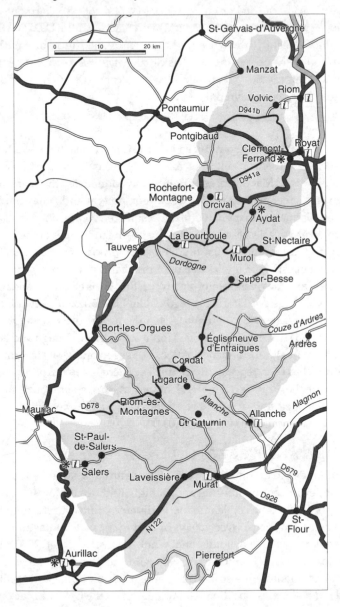

Park HQ. Maison du Parc, Château de Montlosier, près Randanne, 63970 Aydat (☎ 73.65.67.19), closed weekends. It is 20 km from Clermont-Ferrand by the N89 and D5. There are park information centres in Aurillac, 10 rue du Président Delzons (☎ 71.48.68.68); Clermont-Ferrand, 28 rue St-Esprit (☎ 73.92.42.42) and Salers, off the D922 north of Aurillac. Recently a new centre has been opened in Issoir south of Clermont-Ferrand on the N9 beside the *hypermarché* Continent to provide information for two parks – Volcans d'Auvergne and its eastern neighbour, Livradois-Forez.

FAUNA

Chamois have been reintroduced into the Cantal area in the south and *mouflons* (wild sheep) into the massifs of Sancy and Cantal. In the forests of Puy Mary, Bort-les-Orgues and Montlosier there are wild boar, stag, deer and the nocturnal badger, polecat and genet. Smaller mammals such as marten, red fox, red squirrel, weasel and stoat, and many lizard species, can be seen in the green landscapes at the foot of the cratered mountains. Ten hidden *havres de paix* in the park shelter otter colonies; the many lakes have trout, carp, perch, pike, char and crayfish; and the rivers salmon and trout. Birdlife is extensive and birds of prey include red kite, short-toed eagle, little buzzard, kestrel, goshawk, peregrine falcon and owl. Also look for the black woodpecker, red-backed shrike, golden oriole, Montagu's harrier, chough and great tit. The annual transhumance of flocks of sheep and goats to summer pastures has been repeated for centuries. There is a *parc zoologique* just south of the Puy de Dôme and others at Ardes-sur-Couze in the Cézallier area and at Murat, La Maison de la Faune, which is an *ecomusée* of local wildlife (☎ 71.20.03.80).

FLORA AND VEGETATION

Woodlands are dominated by oak at low altitudes, sweet chestnut in the valleys, beech on hillsides and, at high altitudes, fir forests such as the Col de Guéry. The landscape is diverse, from barren mountain craters to peat bogs, river valleys and verdant plateau pastures carpeted with yellow daffodils and white narcissus. Over 2000 plant species can be seen in the park with wild orchids, blue violets, herb Paris, anemones, blue sow thistle, Welsh poppy, spikenard, gentian and red helleborine. At Riom-ès-Montagnes on the D678 La Maison de la Gentiane et de la Flore has a botanic garden and exhibition of medicinal plants, open June–Sept. (☎ 71.78.10.45). At St-Alyre-ès-Montagne et Compains on the D36 south of Besse is the Tourbières (peat bogs) *ecomusée*.

WHAT TO DO

Walks. The Grande Randonnée 4 starts in the southeast at St-Flour and moves west to the Plomb de Cantal and Puy Mary, then north to St-Saturnin and Condat, through the Monts Dore, Puy de Sancy and Mont Losier and exits in the northwest at Pontgibaud. The GR 30 is called the *Tour des Lacs d'Auvergne* and is concentrated around the Monts Dore and includes the Lacs de Guéry, Servière, Chambon and Aydat. The Maison du Parc is a good start point. The GR 441 is called the *Tour de la Chaine des Puys* and is concentrated around the Monts Dômes with Volvic in the north and Saulzet-le-Froid in the south. The GR 33 is called *La Combraille aux Monts du Forez*. It comes in from the northwest at St-Pierre-Roche, runs southeast via Puy de Mercoeur to the Montagne de la Serre and St-Amant, turns south to Puy de St Sandoux north of Champix, and then goes east towards the nature park of Livradois-Forez. The GR 41 goes from Brioude and Bresle in the southeast corner, works its way west through the Cézallier over Le Luguet, and turns north to Compains, Puy de Montchal, Super-Besse and Puy de Sancy towards La Bourboule on the western park boundary. The GR 400 called *Sentier des Volcans du Cantal* is a figure of eight route between Murat in the southeast and St-Paul-de-Salers in the southwest around the edges of the Monts du Cantal. Lastly a circular *Tour du Cézallier* can be started at Allanche, Mazoire, La Godivelle or Marcenat.

Horse-riding. There are *centres équestres* from north to south at Volvic, Nohanent, Ceyssat, Puy de Sancy, Bort-les-Orgues, Apchat, St-Vincent, St-Martin-Valmeroux and Vic-sur-Cère.

Cycling/VTT. This is very popular and a *randonnée cyclo-touriste* called *L'Etoile des Cimes Auvergnates* has been marked out. Cycles can be hired in the park as well as from SNCF stations.

Canoe/kayak/sailing. Facilities available at most of the 15 park lakes.

In the Puy de Dôme, northern half, at Lacs d'Aydat, Chambon, de Guéry, Pavin and Super-Besse. In the Cantal, southern half, at Lanobre/Bort-les-Orgues, Lac Crégut at Lastioules and Lac du Pêcher at Allanche. Advice from Park HQ or tourist offices.

Skiing. There are over 40 ski centres mostly for *ski de fond* or *ski nordique*, i.e. cross-country. The main *ski alpin stations classés* are at Le Mont-Dore and Super-Besse. There is a ski museum at Besse-en-Chandesse, and Chambon-des-Neiges, Chastreix-Sancy, La Tour-Sancy and St-Anthème-Prabourée are official ski centres. Ask for skiing leaflet from Park HQ.

WHAT TO SEE

Natural sights. There are so many that choice is invidious, but certainly try to see Lac Davin, the massif of Sancy and the summits of Puy de Dôme and Puy de Pariou.

Châteaux. See the park leaflet *Route des Châteaux d'Auvergne*. In the park itself from north to south, the best are the 13–17thC Chazeron near Châtelguyon; Tournoël, 12–16thC, 8 km north of Clermont-Ferrand; Château-Dauphin at Pontgibaud; Cordes, 15thC, at Orcival: Murol, 12–16thC, at St-Nectaire; La Batisse, 15–18thC, at Chanonat; St-Saturnin, 13–15thC; La Boyle, 14thC, at Brézon; with others at Murat, Chavagnac, Tournemire and Fontanges.

Churches. The best are the basilicas of Notre-Dame-d'Orcival and St-Nectaire. There are another 30 churches and chapels scattered round the park, including St-Saturnin, Allanche and the Abbaye de Megemont. One of the pilgrimage routes to Santiago de Compostela passed through the park, and beautiful churches were built for the pilgrims.

Museums. The Park HQ at the Château de Montlosier has permanent and temporary exhibitions about *volcanisme* and the Auvergne. In Volvic the Maison de la Pierre (closed Tue.) is an *ecomusée* devoted to the study of stone, lava, *volcanisme* and stoneworking with *son et lumière* May–Sept. At Égliseneuve d'Entraigues is the Maison des Fromages d'Auvergne, June–Sept., where you can taste all the Auvergne cheeses and the Auvergne wines of Corent, Châteaugay, Madargue and Chanturgue. The Château de Val at Lanobre near Bort-les-Orgues is a permanent exhibition of local lithographs and paintings. At Laveissière on rte du Lioran is the Maison du Buronnier (local shepherds) where you can see how local cheese is made and then taste it. At Lanobre is the Musée de la Radio et du Phonographe, open Apr.–Sept. At Besse is the Maison de l'Eau et de la Pêche with aquaria, visits to fish enclosures and exhibitions about the rivers, lakes and Auvergne fish species.

Thermal spas. Five of the Auvergne's ten major thermal spas are situated within the park at La Bourboule, Châtelguyon, Le Mont-Dore, Royat-Chamalières and St-Nectaire. Information from tourist offices.

WHERE TO STAY

There are youth hostels in Chambon-sur-Lac, Le Mont-Dore and Clermont-Ferrand, over 20 campsites and many *gîtes d'étape*. *Auberges* and hotels are to be found in the ski centres and in villages within the park. Outside the park larger hotels are to be found in Clermont-Ferrand, Aurillac and Issoire.

TOURIST OFFICES

Puy de Dôme. La Bourboule (☎ 73.81.07.99). Orcival (☎ 73.65.86.34). Murol (☎ 73.88.62.62). Royat (☎ 73.35.81.87). Volvic (☎ 73.33.50.38). *Cantal.* Aurillac (☎ 71.48.46.58). Allanche (☎ 71.20.41.84). Murat (☎ 71.20.09.47). Salers (☎ 71.40.72.33). Riom (☎ 71.78.07.37).

REGIONAL VISITS

Aurillac to see the Château St-Étienne and Maison des Volcans.
St-Flour has an interesting cathedral and museums.
Brioude to see the Basilique St-Julien.
Vichy, north of Clermont-Ferrand, to see France's No. 1 spa town.
Issoire has the old abbey of St-Austremoine.

LIVRADOIS-FOREZ

Region: AUVERGNE

Created recently in 1983, this park is in the eastern sector of the Auvergne, parallel to its sister park of Volcans. East and southeast of Clermont-Ferrand it extends to 297,000 ha with 163 communes and 105,000 inhabitants spread over the Haute-Loire and Puy-de-Dôme *départements*. The main towns are Thiers (pop. 17,000) in the north and Ambert (pop. 8000) in the centre. The major river, the Dore, a tributary of the Allier, meanders south from Vichy through the centre of the park between the Monts du Livradois and Monts du Forez. In the north are the Bois Noirs, in the centre the plain around Ambert and in the south the massif of Chaise-Dieu. The highest peak is Pierre-sur-Haute (1643 m) in the Monts du Forez northeast of Ambert. It is heavily wooded and has three ski slopes, an amusing tourist train, plus traditional papermaking activities and delicious cheeses. Read all about it in the park's newspaper *Gaspard*. Gaspard de Montagne was a famous character from a book/play by Henri Pourrat, and the Olliergues theatre stages this work each August. Mixed farming is important and you will receive a friendly welcome in the *gîtes ruraux*. There are many lakes, and freshwater fish appear on most menus.

Maps. Michelin 73; IGN 49, 50, 2630–4, 2730–4, 2830–4.

Access. From Clermont-Ferrand east by A72/N89 to Thiers. From Thiers south 49 km to Ambert on D906. From Le Puy-en-Velay north by D906 via La Chaise-Dieu to Ambert. Buses go from Thiers south to Ambert, Arlanc and La Chaise-Dieu. SNCF from Clermont-Ferrand via Thiers, south down the river valley parallel to D906 to Ambert and La Chaise-Dieu.

Park HQ. At St-Gervais-sous-Meymont, BP 17, 63880 Olliergues (☎ 73.95.54.31), open all year 0830–1230, 1400–1800. It is situated on the D906 3 km northwest of Olliergues. It sells useful leaflets including *La Route des Métiers* and *Festivités* and four regional guides: *Bas-Livradois-Comté*, *Monts du Forez-Ambert*, *Pays Thiernois* and *Haut-Livradois*. A

PNR Volcans d'Auvergne –
Top: hang-gliding above *La Chaine des Puys* (photo Monestier)
Below left: *Anemona sulphurea*   right: *Soldanelle* (photo P. Rozier)

PNR Volcans d'Auvergne – Top left: *Gentiana lutea*   right: *Aconitum napellum*
(photo Jobertom)   Below: *Lilium martago* (photo L. Perrier)

Carte Foliplus (fee) entitles visitors to discounts on most châteaux visits, festivals, *spectacles*, etc.

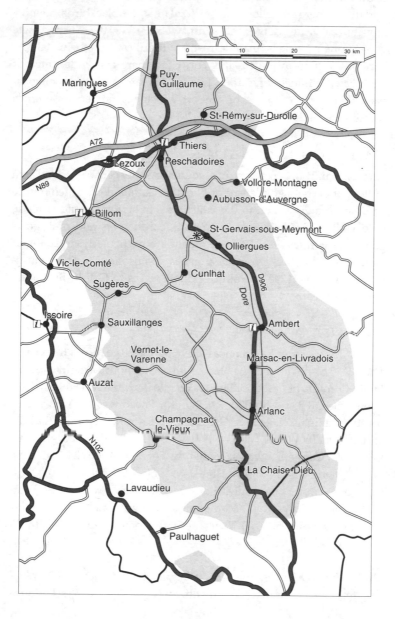

FAUNA

A curious mixture of mammals, reptiles, birds and insects if you can find them. There are yellow and black salamander, blackbirds, hoopoe, grey buzzard, meadow pipit, swift, woodpecker, deer, hedgehogs, grasshoppers, crickets, many unusual butterflies, plus the usual fox, hare and rabbit. In the streams and lakes there is a wide range of freshwater fish including trout, pike and bream. Visit the zoological park of Le Bony southwest of Ambert, which has indigenous animals running free in its 25 ha (☎ 73.82.13.29).

FLORA AND VEGETATION

Forests, mainly of beech and fir, account for 50 per cent of the land area of the park. The high plateau of Forez is heathland on which myrtle and gentians grow, and in the valleys are to be found wild narcissi, blue violas, wild geranium, cranesbill, cornflowers and pink polygonum. The flowers of Puy-St-Romain are particularly notable and include alpine roses, Pyrenean angelica and asphodels. The Hautes-Chaumes above 1200 m from Col-de-Supeyres to Col-du-Béal are a botanist's dream.

WHAT TO DO

Walks. The Grandes Randonnées 3, 33, 330 and 60 go through the park. The GR 33 comes in from the west south of Clermont-Ferrand and past Vic-le-Comté runs east to Olliergues up into the Monts du Forez, where it joins the GR 3 and GR 330, which in turn head west to Ambert and south to La Chaise-Dieu. The GR 3 continues north, keeping in the hills and eventually passing east of Thiers. The walking regions are: Bas-Livradois/Comté, 25 walks; Monts du Forez/Ambert, 24 walks; Le Pays Thiernois, 21 walks; Haut-Livradois, 22 walks. Four local topoguides are on sale locally. There are daily half- or whole-day group walks during July–Aug. accompanied by a guide: Monts du Forez Découverte (☎ 73.95.47.57). There are 500 km of marked bridlepaths in the park.

Horse-riding. *Centres équestres* at Paulhaguet, Celles-sur-Durolle/Chabreloche, Cunlhat, Sermentizon/Courpierre, Peschadoires and Billom. There are 40 altogether. Consult the *Guide de la Cavalée Bleue*.

Pack-horses. Chamina organises activities including *chevaux bâtés*. Ask at Park HQ for details.

Canoe/kayak. Apart from rentals the length of the river Dore, the large *plans d'eau* have facilities at Cunlhat, Vollore-Montagne, Le Vernet-le-Varenne, St-Rémy-sur-Durolle, Arlanc and La Chaise-Dieu.

Cycling/VTT. Park HQ has a free leaflet giving suggested circuits for this popular pursuit. There are *courses* through the summer for amateur cyclists: Centre Cyclo-tourisme, Aubusson d'Auvergne (☎ 73.53.16.94).

Skiing. Centres at La Chaise-Dieu, Allègre, Monts du Forez and Montagne Bourbonnaise in the northeast. Details from Park HQ or ☎ 73.95.20.64.

Aero-club. This is based in Ambert and tourist flights are available.

Tourist train. A special vintage turbo-diesel train with 84 seats and observation cars runs north–south from Pont-de-Dore or Courpière to Ambert or Arlanc during summer weekends. Details from SNCF stations or Park HQ or ☎ 73.82.43.88. The run on the 'Cévenol' down the valley of the Dore river is most attractive across viaducts and through tunnels

WHAT TO SEE

Museums

St-Anthème. Jasserie du Coq Noir (peasant folklore museum).

Ambert. Musée Historique du Papier, Richard-le-Bas (☎ 73.82.03.11). History of local papermaking in a working paper mill.

Arlanc. Musée de la Dentelle (lace) in Mairie (☎ 73.95.00.03).

Thiers. Maison-Musée des Couteliers, 58 rue de la Coutellerie (☎ 73.80.58.86). History of cutlery manufacture in the region.

Marsac-en-Livradois. Musée des Pénitents Blancs (☎ 73.95.60.08). History of local religious art.

Maringues. Musée des Tanneries, 3 rue St-Maurice (☎ 73.68.70.44). History of leatherworking over the ages.

Lezoux. Musée de la Poterie. History of pottery since prehistoric times.

Frugières-le-Pin-Gare southeast of Brioude now has a Musée de la Résistance.

Châteaux

Vollore. 12–17thC in Vollore-Ville 18 km south of Thiers (☎ 73.53.71.06).

Ravel. 13–18thC 7 km from Lezoux (☎ 73.68.44.63).

Montmorin. 12–13thC near Billom (☎ 73.68.30.94).

Martinanches. 11–16thC 25 km south of Thiers (☎ 73.70.80.02).

Chavaniac-Lafayette. 17thC between Brioude and Le Puy (☎ 71.77.50.32).

Busseol. 12thC 20 km southeast of Clermont-Ferrand (☎ 73.69.00.84).

Aulteribe. 15thC 15 km southwest of Thiers (☎ 73.53.14.55).

Churches. The 11thC Abbaye de la Chaise-Dieu and the 14thC Église St-Robert with its famous *danse macabre* painting, in the village of La Chaise-Dieu, are well worth a visit. Others are at Arlanc, Ambert, Champdieu, Courpière, Thiers, Billom, Lavaudieu and the abbey of Montpeyroux north of Thiers.

Concerts. Each summer concerts are held in Thiers, Ambert, Cunlhat and Le Saint-Dieu.

Crafts. The association of Artisans et Paysans du Livradois has a summer exhibition at St-Bonnet-le-Bourg, 1430–1800 in July–Aug. The *fromageries* of the Monts du Forez produce blue cow's milk cheese called *fourmes* – a great delicacy. Local wine can be tasted at Ris during the July–Sept. exhibition of *la vigne et le vin*.

Folklore. Ambert has a three-day festival in late July.

Volcano. The only volcanic crater in the park is the Mont Bar near Allègre in the Massif du Dèves.

Fêtes/fairs. Thiers has a folklore and harvest-meadow fair (*pré*) in mid-Sept. Billom has a summer carnival and a garlic fair, and the *fête* of the bilberry takes place in Col-du-Béal. Ambert has a *marionnette* summer season, Vollore castle has summer concerts and La Chaise-Dieu has a prestigious musical festival in last week Aug. Every village has an end-of-summer *fête*. Details from tourist offices.

WHERE TO STAY

The Park HQ has a list of campsites, *gîtes*, holiday villages and hostels. Thiers and Ambert have a number of modest hotels.

TOURIST OFFICES

Ambert (☎ 73.82.61.90). Arlanc (☎ 73.95.11.15). Billom (☎ 73.68.39.85). La Chaise-Dieu (☎ 71.00.01.16). Thiers at Château du Pirou (☎ 73.80.10.74). Le Puy, 12 rue Philippe-Jourde (☎ 71.09.26.05).

REGIONAL VISITS

North to Vichy to take the waters, southeast to see the spectacular town of Le Puy-en-Velay with its cathedral, *vieille ville*, museum and cloisters. The municipal tourist office in Clermont-Ferrand has a detailed car circuit of 250 km leaving by the N9, which takes in practically all of 50 sights in and around the nature park.

PILAT

Region: RHÔNE VALLEY

Surprisingly, this small regional park of 65,000 ha situated between the large industrial town of St-Étienne and the Rhône valley has become well known in France. The park management decided that since their Grandes Randonnées and nine local walks were so practical and popular they would make Le Pilat a VTT centre. The championship of France, the Rallye du Parc du Pilat, is held here, usually in early Sept., over a 22 km circuit near Tarentaise. Hundreds of cycles are owned by the park and are now hired out by ten *loueurs*, much to the physical benefit of 200,000 cyclists and the financial benefit of scores of local hoteliers, restaurateurs and craftspeople. There is no record of what the walkers or the local fauna feel about this invasion! But during the rest of the year the park is a delight. It consists of the Pilat mountains extending northwards from the Cévennes. The highest peaks are the Crêt de la Perdrix (1432 m) on Mont Pilat, L'Oeillon and Le Grand Bois. On the summits are great granite boulders known as *chirats*. Streams and small rivers such as the Couzon, Dorlay, Regrillon, Gier and Furan feed into the Loire or Rhône through extensive gorges. Founded in 1974, the park has 45 communes with 39,000 inhabitants in the *départements* of Rhône and Loire. Nestling in the heavily wooded mountains which make up two-thirds of the park are a score of villages including Condrieu, Pélussin and Bourg-Argental which are reached by winding roads. *Reader's Digest* has stated that Ste-Croix-en-Jarez is the *'plus beau village de France'*. The park has a distinctly athletic profile with 350 km of trails, 8 skiing villages, canoe/kayak, horse-riding, orienteering, climbing, etc. But still wild boar, red and roe deer, migrating birds and river fish manage to survive, even thrive. And on the east side where the park extends to the Rhône valley orchards and vineyards flourish.

Maps. Michelin 74, 76, 77; IGN 51.

Access. From St-Étienne southeast by N82 and D8 amid spectacular scenery. From Lyon southwest by D42/D502. From Vienne southwest by N86 to Condrieu. From Annonay northwest by N82. SNCF to

St-Étienne (TGV). Local buses from St-Étienne and from Annonay. Air Inter fly to St-Étienne; the airport is at St-Étienne Bouthéon.

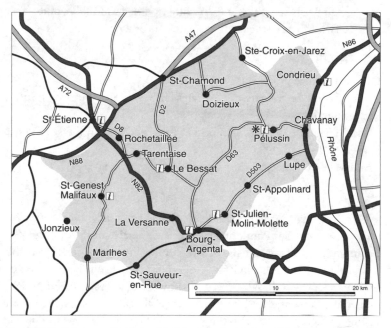

Park HQ. Maison du Parc, Le Moulin de Virieu, BP 17, 2 rue Benaÿ, 42410 Pélussin (☎ 74.87.65.24), closed weekends. It has an excellent range of literature. The small town of Pélussin is on the D7 off the N86 in the northeast corner of the park, quite close to the Rhône.

FAUNA

Among the chestnut forests of Terrasse-sur-Dolay and Pavezin and the hills of Roizey and Pélussin roam wild boar. Also on the wooded hills many red and roe deer can be seen, and on the Malleral heights wild sheep in the Parc au Mouflon. Over 100 bird species have been noted including crag martin, rock swallow, Bonelli's eagle, citril finch and, in the autumn, migrant flocks on their journey south down the Rhône valley. Hunting and fishing activities are regulated. Insect life flourishes with many varieties of dragonfly, and freshwater fish include salmon, loach, fario trout and perch.

FLORA AND VEGETATION

Above 800 m are pine, fir and beech woods, and in the lowlands expect to see sweet chestnut, white oak, ash, poplar and wild cherry. Alpine flowers flourish together with orchids, wild daffodils, aconite and arnica. Two-thirds of the park area consists of woodland.

ECOMUSÉES

Not particularly grand but worth a look.

La Maison de la Béate in L'Allier-Marlhes, in the southwest, July–Sept., Sun. only.

La Maison de la Passementerie at Jonzieux, also in the southwest corner.

La Maison de la Gabelle, northwest of Condrieu.

WHAT TO DO

Walks. There is a local topoguide available: *Les Neuf grands sentiers du Parc*. The Grande Randonnée 7 passes north–south through St-Chamond, Le Bessat and Le Traco, coming in to the park from the southwest at the Col du Grand Bois (N82) and leaving northeast of St-Étienne. The GR 42 passes northwest–southeast through Rochetaillée, Le Bessat and Bourg-Argental. Local walks are signed in orange/blue stripes, such as the Tour de la Loire of 150 km, and minor walks are marked by yellow/white stripes.

Horse-riding. There are seven *centres équestres* at Pélussin, St-Julien-Molin-Molette, Farnay, Colombier-sous-Pilat, St-Genest-Malifaux and Le Guizay.

Orienteering. Courses are run by the Club Orient Express, 42 Les Gouettets, Pélussin (☎ 74.87.62.75).

Cycling/VTT. Among the ten bicycle renters are Foyer de Ski at Le Bessat, St-Régis-du-Coin and Rivory Sports in Pélussin, and Maison de l'Eau at Marlhes. Information from Ligue du Forez, 4 rue André-Malraux, 42000 St-Étienne.

Courses. The Maison de l'Eau (Centre Permanent d'Initiation à l'Environment) near Marlhes (☎ 77.51.82.31) offers courses (*stages*) on ecology, vegetation and ornithology. Open Apr.–Sept. 1500–1900.

Canoe/kayak. A large man-made lake at St-Pierre-de-Boeuf off the N86 near the river Rhône offers summer lessons (☎ 74.87.14.50). Also at the Barrage du Dorlay (☎ 77.20.99.73) off the D76, 10 km north of Mont Pilat. Sail-boarding at Condrieu, St-Pierre-de-Boeuf and Les Roches-de-Condrieu on the Rhône (☎ 74.56.30.53).

Climbing. There are two official rock faces. Roche Corbières is near Rochetaillée and Gouffre d'Enfer is off the D8 4 km east of St-Étienne. Doizieux at Les Scies is off the D120 3 km northwest of Mont Pilat. Information from Club Alpin Français, 26 rue Marengo, St-Étienne (☎ 77.38.25.37).

Fishing. You need a permit. Apply to Club des Pêcheurs Sportifs, Forez Velay, 15 rue Dormoy, St-Étienne or Fédération de Pêche de la Loire, 12 rue d'Arcade, St-Étienne.

Leisure centres (*bases de loisirs*). One is at St-Pierre-de-Boeuf (☎ 74.87.14.50) and another at Condrieu (☎ 74.56.52.22).

Swimming. Open-air *baignades* are at St-Sauveur-en-Rue on the river Déome and at Condrieu, St-Pierre-de-Boeuf and St-Julien-Molin-Molette on the river Ternay. A large swimming-pool at Pélussin is open June–Sept.

Skiing. There are eight villages in the park with marked pistes (*ski de fond*) for winter skiing: Le Bessat, Tarentaise, St-Régis-du-Coin, Bardigues, Marlhes, St-Genest-Malifaux, Jonzieux and La Versanne. For bookings ☎ 77.20.43.43. More sophisticated *ski de piste* is available at La Jasserie and Graix, each with two *téléskis*. Information from Allo-neige (☎ 77.20.43.43).

Hang-gliding (*delta-plane*). Sites are at Col de Pavezin, Collet de Doizieux and Le Crêt de l'Oeillon.

Fairs/fêtes. Bourg-Argental has a spring cheese fair; Pélussin an apple fair on 11 Nov.; Chavannay a wine market in Dec.; and Malleval a spring vignerons' festival.

WHAT TO SEE

Natural sights. There are a number of photogenic sights including Le Crêt de l'Oeillon on Mont Pilat with views over the mountains of the Auvergne to the south and the Alps to the east. The Gouffre d'Enfer to the south of Rochetaillée, the gorges of Malleval near Lupe and the gorges of the river Furan 7 km east of St-Étienne are all spectacular. The Saut du Gier near Valla-en-Gier off D2 10 km south of St-Chamond, the dams (*barrages*) of Sapt and Gouffre d'Enfer, and the lakes between St-Régis-du-Coin and Col de la République all give scope for splendid photographs.

Châteaux. Grillet, which has super wines, near La Chapelle-Villars; Virieu near the Maison du Parc at Pélussin; La Terrasse-sur-Dorlay; and Malleval, which is an interesting ruin.

Churches. The ancient Chartreuse monastery founded in the 13thC in the beautiful rectangular village of Ste-Croix-en-Jarez 13 km northwest of Condrieu should be visited. Others of note include the Chapelle (and Château) of Bourg-Argental, the church at St-Appolinard and the priory at Roisy.

Illuminations. There are four attractive places illuminated on summer evenings – Malleval, Ste-Croix-en-Jarez, La Rochetaillée and Doizieux.

WHERE TO STAY

There are campsites within the park at Bourg-Argental, St-Julien-Molin-Molette, St-Pierre-de-Boeuf, Pélussin and Condrieu. There are also many *gîtes* and *chambres d'hôte* – details from tourist offices. There are pleasant little *auberges* in Pélussin, Bourg-Argental, Bessat, Jonzieux, Marlhes, Ste-Croix-en-Jarez and Colombier.

TOURIST OFFICES

Bourg-Argental, on N82 (☎ 77.39.63.49) – summer only.
Pélussin. Mairie (☎ 74.87.28.51) – summer only.
St-Genest-Malifaux. Mairie (☎ 77.51.20.01) – summer only.

Condrieu on N86. Mairie (☎ 74.59.50.38) – summer only.
Le Bessat. Maison Communale (☎ 77.20.43.76) – open all year.
Val du Ternay. St-Julien-Molin-Molette, Bourg-Argental (☎ 77.52.63.49)
   – summer only.
St-Étienne. 12 rue Gérentet (☎ 77.25.12.14) – open all year.

REGIONAL VISITS

Parc Ornithologique de la Dombes, 01330 Villars-les-Dombes (☎
79.80.05.54) is 50 km northeast of the park and 30 km north of Lyon. It
is worth a detour to see a 20 ha park with many lakes on which are 350
local bird species with 2000 birds permanently resident, plus migrants.

St-Étienne has four museums of note – Modern Art, Art and Industry, Arms and Weapons, and Beaux-Arts, plus botanical gardens near
the Maison de la Culture.

Vercors Nature Park is 50 km southeast.

Vienne (20 km northeast) is more interesting than St-Étienne, with
the cathedral of St-Maurice, the church and cloisters of St-André-le-
Bas, and a Roman theatre and temple of Augustus.

VERCORS

Region: DAUPHINÉ ALPS

A magnificent sub-alpine region lies between the towns of Valence, Die and Grenoble straddling the *départements* of Isère and Drôme. It is a satisfying blend of northern Provence, with vines, lavender and walnut growing, and mountain pastures with alpine flowers and fauna. Most of the park of 135,000 ha is on a high limestone plateau with many caves which made it a centre of the World War II resistance movement. Half the area is under forest cover of pine, but nevertheless there are strikingly beautiful natural formations of peaks over 2000 m, cliffs and gorges such as those of the Bourne, Nan and Gervanne, caves and grottoes, underground streams and the largest nature reserve in France. The park is 55 km long from north to south and is up to 40 km wide; the Rhône valley lies to the west, the Isère to the north, the Drôme to the south and the Drac to the east. Around the Grand Veymont mountain is the Vercors Hauts-Plateaux reserve where 20,000 sheep graze before transhumance shepherds lead them down to the valleys. There are five natural regions within the park: around Die to the south, Royans-Coulmes to the west, Trièves to the east, Quatre Montagnes to the north and the nature reserve in the southeast. The population of 26,000 in 62 communes is mainly engaged in forestry, agriculture, craft industries and tourism. It is one of the most sporting of the French nature parks with 2850 km of marked paths and 1200 km of ski pistes and trails. Features of interest include prehistoric sites, a resistance museum, a Cistercian abbey, hanging houses at Pont-en-Royans, grottoes and the vineyards around Die in which the well-known Clairette wine can be tasted.

Maps. Michelin 77; IGN 52, 226–9.

Access. 10 km by road from Grenoble south on N75. From Valence east to Die by D111/D93. From Sisteron north by N93 or N75. SNCF stations at Grenoble, Valence and Die. Airports are at Grenoble-Vercors and Valence-Chabeuil. There are many buses from Grenoble or Valence towards the park.

70

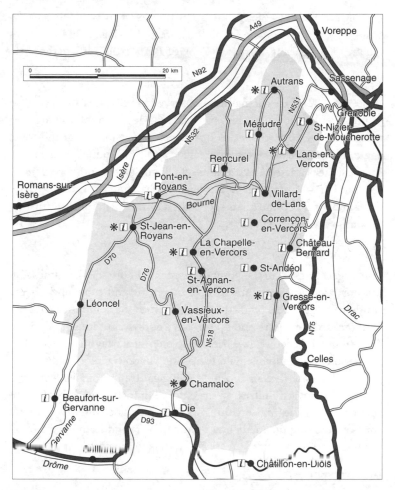

Park HQ. Maison du Parc, chemin des Fusillés, BP 14, 38250 Lans-en-Vercors (☎ 76.95.40.33). It is reached by the N531 from the western outskirts of Grenoble. Excellent literature is available including a free schematic map of the park. There are also additional sources of information. (1) La Maison du Parc et de la Spéléologie (potholing), 26420 La Chapelle-en-Vercors (☎ 75.48.22.38) is right in the centre of the park at the junction of the N518 and D103. (2) La Maison du Parc et de la Flore, Chamaloc (☎ 75.22.11.82) is on the N518 north of Die. (3) La Maison du Parc et du Royans, rue Pasteur, 26190 St-Jean-en-Royans (☎

75.48.70.59) is on the west side of the park on the D76. (4) La Maison du Parc et du Trièves, 38650 Gresse-en-Vercors (☎ 76.34.10.98) is on the east side of the park on the D8 off the N75. (5) La Maison du Parc et des Quatre Montagnes at Autrans (☎ 76.95.35.01) is in the north of the park.

FAUNA

Among the 32 species of mammal observed are chamois, ibex, *mouflon* (wild sheep), wild boar, stag, red and roe deer, mountain hare and marmot. Over 80 bird species have been noted including the royal eagle, Grand-Duc owl, peregrine falcon and capercaillie (*grand tétras*). The best areas are the Col du Rousset (chamois), around Varces (*mouflon*) and the Massif des Coulmes (*mouflon*, stag and deer). Many thousands of sheep and goats spend the summer in the park, returning to southern Provence in Sept.

FLORA AND VEGETATION

The largest forests are the Forêt de Lente and Forêt des Coulmes. On the north-facing slopes are spruce, beech, fir and pine, and on the southern slopes Scots pine and downy oak. In the southern sector are fruit orchards of cherry and apple, olive and walnut trees, and vines. The mountain pastures are rich in plants – martagon lilies, lady's slipper orchids, gentians, wild tulips, dog's-tooth violets and *sabot de Vénus*. There are five signposted ecological trails from Vassieux-en-Vercors, Chamaloc, Prélenfrey-du-Guà, Choranche and St-Nizier-du-Moucherotte. The Maison du Parc at Chamaloc offers week-long courses studying the medicinal plants to be found in the park. In all there are 1800 different plant species native to the park.

WHAT TO DO

Walks. There are 2850 km of signposted paths. The Grande Randonnée 9 starts at Saillans on the D93 halfway between Crest and Die, heads north following the Gervanne valley to the Col de la Portette across the Gorges de la Bourne and the valley of Drevenne to Autrans, continues north and leaves the park near Voreppe. The derivatives are 91, 92, 93, 94 and 95, which are mainly west to east. Thematic walks are organised from Autrans, Corrençon, Gresse, Lans, Méaudre, Monestier and Villars, usually from May–Oct. Local topoguides are available.

Horse-riding. There are 800 km of bridlepaths and *centres équestres* are located at Autrans, Villars, Corrençon, Chichilianne, Chelles, Presles, Rochechinard, Gresse, Vassieux, Lans, La Chapelle, Recoubeau and Die.

Cycling/VTT. Rentals and itineraries from Monestier-la-Chapelle and Villars. Consult the Maisons du Parc.

Caving. Courses from Maison de la Spéléologie at La Chapelle-en-Vercors.

Climbing. There are several rock faces including Presles. Advice from Maisons du Parc.

Archaeology. From the Maison du Parc at St-Jean-de-Royans there is a 12 km walk to see the prehistoric site and excavations at Chotanche. See also the Musée du Site Préhistorique at Vassieux-en-Vercors (☎ 75.48.27.81).

Skiing. There are over 23 ski runs and resorts with 300 km of alpine pistes and 900 km of cross-country ski trails across the Massif du Vercors. The main resorts are Villard-de-Lans (☎ 76.95.03.30) and Corrençon-en-Vercors (☎ 76.95.82.26). They are situated in the northeast corner of the park off the N531. There are 20 modest village resorts which may be more fun. Ask Maisons du Parc for their advice.

Fishing. Trout angling is possible in the mountain lakes, rivers and streams. Information from Maisons du Parc.

Canoe/kayak. The Maisons du Parc will advise about the best rivers, rental, etc., along the Gorges de la Bourne.

WHAT TO SEE

Museums. At Lans-en-Vercors on the rte de Villard is the 'magic' Automates museum with 200 animated *personnages* (☎ 76.95.40.14). In Vassieux is the museum dedicated to the gallant Maquis de Vercors who died in their hundreds in 1942–4 (☎ 75.48.28.46). There are memorial cemeteries in Vassieux and St-Nizier. A dozen villages were destroyed by the Nazis. At Villard-de-Lans is the Maison du Patrimonie (☎ 76.95.17.31) with folklore deriving from 200 local families in Canton des Quatre Montagnes. In Royans are the remains of a medieval castle and the Musée Mémoire de Rochechinard (☎ 75.48.62.53) with local folklore and costume. Others are the Dauphins' museum at Beauvoir-en-Royans and the Protestantism museum at Die.

Jardin Ferroviaire. From Mar.–Nov. a miniature railway chugs for 1 km around large gardens, between Chatte and St-Marcelin, rte de Lyon (☎ 76.38.54.55).

Bateau-mouche. At St-Nazaire-en-Royans is a paddle-steamer which cruises for 1½ hours in the valley of the Bourne through 220 ha of canal and rivers (☎ 75.48.45.76).

Historic sites. The 12thC Cistercian monastery at Léoncel is reached by the Gorges de la Bourne, then through St-Jean-en-Royans south on the D70. In Die the 12thC cathedral of Notre-Dame is worth a visit. At Le Moucherotte is the delightful little mountain chapel of St-Nizier, built in the 11thC.

Mountains. The north–south massif running from St-Nizier through Le Moucherotte (1901 m), La Grande Moucheville (2285 m) and Le Grand Veymont (2341 m) is quite spectacular, as is Mont Aiguille (2095 m), which is surmounted by huge white chalk vertical rocks, making it a difficult rock face to climb.

Grottoes. There are ten in various parts of the park. The Choranches, with a subterranean lake and *son et lumière*, are the best known. Before a visit ask for advice from Maisons du Parc.

Crafts. In eight park villages there are skilled craftspeople making walnut wine, ceramics, wooden toys, paintings on silk, ironwork, pottery and sculpture. The Maisons du Parc will advise you.

Wine tour. Visit the Cave Cooperative in Die to see a range of local wines including Clairette and vin de Châtillon. In the hamlet of St-Ro-

mans there is a small tourist *train des vignes* (☎ 75.40.53.98). The still
and sparkling white wines are well worth buying.

Pretty villages. Pont-en-Royans in the northwest of the park has a
score of old houses suspended above the river Bourne – very pretty
and photogenic. Châtillon in the south, east of Die, is an unspoilt
medieval village with narrow *ruelles* (lanes).

Panorama 2000. A magnificent panorama from Villard-de-Lans by
télécabine up the mountain to Côte 2000 above the ski slopes with views
to Mont Aigoual (Parc National des Cévennes) and the crater tops of
the Jura mountains. Walk down by signed path. ☎ 76.95.15.43.

WHERE TO STAY

There are 15 *refuges* for walkers in the park, 23 campsites and youth
hostels (OCCAJ) at Autrans, Mont-de-Lans and Villars. There are
auberges and small hotels in a dozen villages including Die, Pont-en-
Royans, Villard-de-Lans, La Chapelle-en-Vercors and St-Nazaire-en-
Royans.

TOURIST OFFICES

Quatre Montagnes region. Autrans (☎ 76.95.30.70); Corrençon-en-Ver-
    cors (☎ 75.95.81.75); Lans-en-Vercors (☎ 76.95.42.62); Méaudre (☎
    75.95.20.68); St-Nizier-du-Moucherotte (☎ 76.53.40.60); Villard-de-
    Lans (☎ 76.95.10.38).
Trièves region. Château-Bernard (☎ 76.72.38.31); Gresse-en-Vercors (☎
    76.34.33.40); St-Andéol (☎ 76.34.00.80).
Vercors-Central. La Chapelle-en-Vercors (☎ 75.48.22.54); Vassieux-en-
    Vercors (☎ 75.48.27.40); St-Agnan-en-Vercors (☎ 75.48.22.21).
Royans-Central. St-Jean-en-Royans (☎ 75.48.61.39); Pont-en-Royans (☎
    76.36.09.10); Rencurel (☎ 76.38.97.29).
Die region. Die (☎ 75.22.03.03); Châtillon-en-Diois (☎ 75.21.10.07);
    Beaufort-sur-Gervanne (☎ 75.76.45.49).

REGIONAL VISITS

Grenoble to see the old town, river Drac promenade, Palais de Justice,
Fort de la Bastille, St-Laurent church and several museums.

Valence to see the cathedral, Maison des Têtes, Champ de Mars and museum.

Romans-sur-Isère to see St-Barnard church, museums and promenades along the river Isère.

Sassenage on N532 northwest of Grenoble to see the château and wine *chais*, reputed to be one of the seven wonders of the Dauphiné region.

St-Pierre-de-Chartreuse on D512 north of Grenoble to see the fabulous old Convent de la Grande Chartreuse with its La Correrie (Carthusian museum). Best visited during the week.

VANOISE

Region: SAVOY ALPS

The first national nature park in France was created in 1963 for a noble reason. Since 1936 alpine ibex had been protected across the Italian border in the park of Grand-Paradis. But when ibex came innocently west across the border in search of pasture they ended up as part of the excellent French cuisine! It may have taken 27 years to establish a park in Savoie with 14 km shared with Italy to protect wildlife, but the current population of 700 ibex are now relatively safe.

This alpine park with mountains rising up to 3800 m consists of a central zone of 53,000 ha between the high valleys of the rivers Arc in the south and Isère in the northwest. Together the Vanoise and the Italian Grand-Paradis constitute the largest reserve in Europe. In the outer zone of 145,000 ha there are 28 communes with 30,000 inhabitants, but no one lives in the heart of the park. Mountain pastures account for 32,000 ha, glaciers and rocks for 20,000. Forests are rare and glacial lakes are many, including the large Glacier de la Vanoise in the centre. This is the most northerly of the four French alpine parks and it has most of the famous ski resorts on or within its boundaries, such as Val-d'Isère, Courchevel and Les Arcs. No road actually crosses the park. The N6, D902, N90 and D915 are good roads but effectively form the boundaries. Nevertheless there are 500 km of marked footpaths and a whole range of sporting activities. The delightful fauna and flora result from a complex rock structure – a geologist's delight. The central zone around the Col de la Vanoise consists of calcareous schistous, quartzite and gypsum rocks, with 107 summits exceeding 3000 m including the Val-d'Isère, Tignes and Grand Sassière nature reserves. Apart from the well-known ski centres, the towns on the periphery include Bourg-St-Maurice, Moutiers, Modane and Lanslebourg-Mont-Cenis.

Maps. Michelin 74; IGN 53, 3532–4, 3632, 3633.

Access. From Chambéry eastwards via Montmelian, N90 north to Albertville and N90 southeast to Moutiers. From Megève southwest on N212 to Albertville and N90 to Moutiers. From Briançon northwest on N91. D902 north and N6 east to Modane. SNCF stations at Moutiers, Landry, Modane and Bourg-St-Maurice. Local buses from those towns.

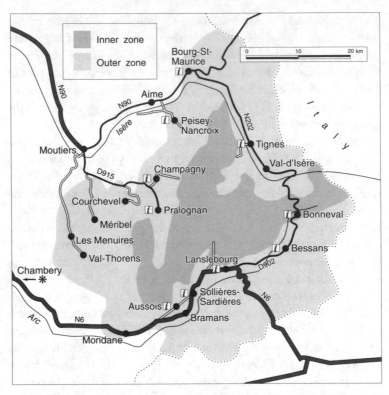

Park HQ. Not very logical, but the Maison du Parc is at 135 rue du Docteur-Julliand, Chambéry (☎ 79.62.30.54). It is difficult to find in Chambéry and it is over 100 km by road west of the park! In practice consult the local tourist offices for advice.

FAUNA

Apart from the colony of 700 ibex, the largest in France, there are 5000 chamois, thousands of marmot, fox, badger, pine and stone martens, mountain hare and smaller mammals such as field voles, fieldmice, stoats and long-eared and pipistrelle bats. Some of the best places to see larger game, preferably at dawn, are the craters of La Valette and Argentine, the schists above the Vallonet, Pont de la Pêche or the Col de l'Aussois and the three nature reserves. Over 125 species of bird have been identified including golden eagle, buzzard, black grouse, capercaillie, ring ouzel, woodpecker, redpoll and Tengmalm owl. In the forest are chaffinches and dunnocks, on the high grasslands thrush, wheatear, waterpipits and rooks, and above the snow line snow finch, alpine accentor and ptarmigan. The Park HQ is, however, worried about the diminution of the capercaillie (*grand tétras*). The birds of prey target water salamanders (*triton alpestre*), rush toads, russet frogs, lizards, esculape snakes and adders. In high summer the park is alive with butterflies such as the mountain clouded yellow, Cynthia's fritillary, scarce copper, large apollo and the alpine Rosalie. In July the park arranges ornithological trails from Termignon, Bessans and Bonneval.

FLORA AND VEGETATION

The forests are mainly coniferous – spruce, fir, larch, Scots pine, mountain pine and arolla pine are widespread. At the sub-alpine level of 1500–2000 m expect to find rhododendron, bilberry and juniper. Among the quartzite and schistous rocks there will be blue-spiked rampion, rock campion, wavy hairgrass, blue thistle (*reine des Alpes*) and round-leaved rest-harrow. Many alpine plants at their best in summer are crocus, violet trumpet gentian, primula, campanula, lady's slipper orchid, yellow anemone, saxifrage and glacier buttercup. In July the park organises botanical expeditions from Pralognan, Aussois, Orgère (Villardin-Berger) and Fornet (Val-d'Isère).

WHAT TO DO

Walks. There are 500 km of marked walks leaving from villages, stations and the valleys. Most of the walks are practicable from June end Oct. The Grande Randonnée 5 arrives from the north, to the west of Bourg-St-Maurice, links up with GR 57 which crosses the N90, ascends to the ski-slopes of La Plagne, straggles southwest across the D915 and then follows the valley of the Belleville to Les Menuires south over Mont Bréguin towards the nature park of Écrins. Meanwhile the GR 5 after La Plagne heads east to Val-d'Isère and southwest to Lanslebourg, having spawned the GR 55 which meanders round the centre of the park. Local walks with guides are available from Pralognan, Peisey-Nancroix, Champagny, Aime, Montalbert, Val-Cenis and Bonneval. The Office National des Forêts offers free short guided tours.

Major walks are the *tour des Glaciers* in four days; the tour of Mont Pourri to spot fauna in two days; and the Mont Pourri tour of six days. Overnight stays in some of the 42 *refuges*. Fee.

Horse-riding. There are *centres équestres* at Bessans, Aussois, Bramans and Termignon in the Maurienne (southern sector) and at all the ski stations in the northern sector, known as Tarentaise.

Geology. Four *tables géologiques* have been placed at Mont Bochor (Pralognan-la-Valoise), Plan du Lac (Termignon), Rosuel (Peisey-Nancrois) and near the Col de l'Iseran (D 902 near Val-d'Isère). From these *tables* one can study the various rock formation strata. Triassic and Jurassic strata have produced famous sites for molluscs and fossil fish.

Safari photos. Organised tours for photographers from Les Menuires, Peisey-Nancroix or Val-d'Isère.

Fishing. Many rivers, streams and the lakes of Aussois, Bramans and Lanslebourg contain trout and other freshwater fish. Check at the tourist offices to see if a local permit is required.

Skiing. Les Trois Vallées is the name given to the famous ski resort areas in Courchevel, Méribel and Les Menuires/Val-Thorens in the western sector of the park southeast of Moutiers, in the eastern sector around Val-d'Isère and in the northern sector at Les Arcs and La Plagne. The Vanoise park offers the finest skiing holidays in France. Consult your travel agent or local tourist office.

Ski stations: Courchevel (☎ 79.08.00.29); Méribel (☎ 79.08.60.01); Les Menuires (☎ 79.00.73.00); Val-Thorens (☎ 79.00.08.08); Val d'Isère (☎ 79.06.10.83; Les Arcs (☎ 79.07.48.00); La Plagne (☎ 79.09.02.01).

WHAT TO SEE

Chapels. St-Sébastien at Lanslevillard, St-Antoine at Bessans with 15thC frescoes, the chapel at Aussois and St-Pierre-d'Extravache at Bramans are worth a visit.

Museums. The archaeological museum at Sollières-Envers is the only one in the park. Chambéry has two – Musée Savoisien (regional history) and Musée d'Histoire Naturelle.

Transhumance. In the first week of Sept. huge sheep flocks leave the mountains at Ugine to return to the valley pastures, often a long distance away.

Crafts. At Bonneval, Sardières, Aussois, Séez and Bessans local craftsmen produce leather goods, pottery and woven or knitted garments.

WHERE TO STAY
There are youth hostels at Lanslebourg, Séez and St-Jean-de-Maurienne, and 42 *refuges de montagne* (which should be reserved in midsummer). Two can be reached by car: the Rosuel near Peisey-Nancroix and the Bois at Champagny-le-Haut. In the Maurienne area there are campsites at Aussois, Bramans, Lanslevillard, Sollières-Sardières and Termignon. In the Tarentaise area campsites are at Champagny, Pralognan, Les Menuires, Peisey-Nancrois, Val-d'Isère, Tignes and Séez. There are *centres d'acceuil* of various kinds: with sporting activities (UCPA) at Pralognan, Val-Cenis and Val-d'Isère; for the young (OCCAJ) at Lanslebourg and St-Martin-de-Belleville; for families (VVF) at St-Martin, Aussois and Méribel. The ski resorts have a wide range of hotels and *auberges*.

TOURIST OFFICES
Haute Maurienne area (southwest/southeast). Aussois (☎ 79.20.40.80). Bessans (☎ 79.05.96.52). Sollières-Sardières (☎ 79.20.50.90). Bonneval (☎ 79.05.08.08). Lanslebourg (☎ 79.05.23.66).

Haute-Tarentaise area (northwest/northeast). Champagny (☎ 79.22.09.53). Pralognan (☎ 79.08.71.68). Peisey-Nancroix (☎ 79.07.12.55). Tignes (☎ 79.06.15.55). Bourg-St-Maurice (☎ 79.07.04.92).

REGIONAL VISITS
One can visit towns outside the park such as St-Jean-de-Maurienne to see the cathedral and Chambéry to see the old town, château, cathedral and church of St Pierre de Lémenc.

Aiguilles-Rouges nature reserve lies 8 km north of Chamonix, west of the N506, and is crossed by the GR 5. In an unspoilt area of 50 sq. km there are glaciers, rock cliffs, lakes, peaks up to 3000 m with delightful sub-alpine flora and the usual chamois, ibex and marmot. Alpine birdlife includes swifts, accentors, choughs, nutcrackers, ravens and finches. Stay in the hamlet of Argentière or Chamonix-Mont-Blanc.

Lac d'Annecy is northeast of Chambéry and northwest of Albertville, and at the southern end is the nature reserve of Marais du Bout du Lac d'Annecy at Petit-Lac between the N508 and D909. It is a wildfowl reserve with nesters such as corncrake, teal, curlew, bittern and garganey. Among the many swans are the winter arrivals of pintail, mallard, scaup, goosander and golden-eye.

ÉCRINS

Region: DAUPHINÉ ALPS

The Écrins national park lies between Grenoble, Gap and Briançon, and was established in 1973. Off the beaten track, it is one of the largest of the French national parks, encompasses a superb mountain massif in its core of 92,000 ha and altogether measures 270,000 ha. It is also the highest park, attaining 4102 m (La Barre des Écrins). Rich fauna and flora can be seen amid the superb alpine scenery, and the area is forested by larch around gorges, lakes, glaciers and cirques. The altitude varies between 800 m and 4100 m, with many mountains over 3000 m. The park is bordered by the rivers Durance, Romanche and Drac. In the core zone, apart from Dormillouse, a small hamlet, there are no inhabitants at all (one of the main reasons why the state funds the park!). There are 61 communes – 23 in the *département* of Isère and 38 in the *département* of Hautes-Alpes – with a total of 27,000 inhabitants. Small villages include Orcières (pop. 900), St-Bonnet-en-Champsaur (pop. 1400), St-Firmin (pop. 500), Villar-d'Avens (pop. 200), Vallouise (pop. 500) and Pelvoux (pop. 400). It is known as the *Parc européen de la haute montagne* and in 1989 was awarded the coveted Council of Europe Diploma, Category A, for the important scientific value placed on the diversity of its flora (more than 2000 species) and fauna. In addition it has made an inventory of plant and wildlife heritage on computer database. Surprisingly perhaps, it has excellent visitor facilities and footpaths by which to explore the four regions of the park, which include six nature reserves, all in high valleys.

The four regions are quite diverse. The northern is bounded by the N91, which leads from Le Bourg-d'Oisans past the reservoir of Chambon and follows the river Romanche to the Col du Lautarat. The massif of Champsaur, with the granite hills of L'Aigle, La Maije, La Grande Ruine and many others, towers above the valley. On the slopes grow spruce forests. To the west the rain-laden Atlantic winds encourage forests of copper beech, pine and fir. To the south the breezes from the Mediterranean along the valley of the river Durance influence more pine forests and lavender growth. In the east the alpine winds from the direction of Briançon, cold and dry, encourage the larch woods, blowing up the valleys of the Gyronde, Fournel and Biaysse. The upper

Durance valley is the land of sheep droving. Each year on St John's Day (25 June) shepherds and flocks move up to the mountain pastures for the summer months (the transhumance).

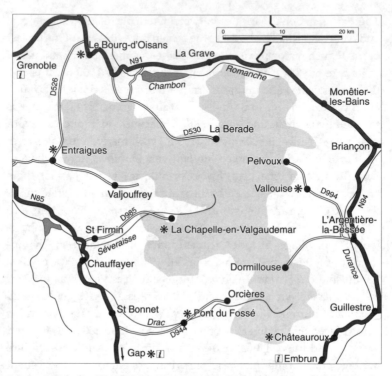

Maps. Michelin 77; IGN 54, 241–3; Didier Richard Alpine Guide No. 6.

Access. From Gap northwards along the Route Napoléon on the N85 over the Col Bayard to the southwest corner of the park. The D944 follows the southern boundary along the river Drac to Orcières. The approach from the southeast is from Lac de Serre-Ponçon, through the town of Embrun on the N94 north to Guillestre (the nature park of Queyras is to the east), and then north to Briançon. From Grenoble in the northwest the D5 and N91 cross along the northern boundary towards Briançon. Minor roads in the park include the D530, D985, D944, D526 and D994. The SNCF line runs between Gap and Briançon. Buses leave Gap for Embrun, Mont Dauphin and St-Crépin.

Park HQ. Service Administratif et Animation, 7 rue du Colonel Roux, BP 142, 05004 Gap (☎ 92.51.40.71). Visited by 200,000 travellers, the park sponsors 54 field workers protecting the environment, grouped into seven sectors: Briançon, L'Oisans, Valbonnais, Valgaudemar, Haut-Champsaur, Embrun and Vallouise. There are seven local Maisons du Parc:

Le Bourg d'Oisans (northwest). Ave. Gambetta, 38520 Le Bourg d'Oisans (☎ 76.80.00.51).

Entraigues (west). Maison Artigues, 38740 Valbonnais (☎ 76.30.20.61).

Briançon (east). Villa Belledonne, 35 bd du Lautaret, 05100 Briançon (☎ 92.21.08.49).

Châteauroux (southeast). Gîtes Communaux, 0538 Châteauroux (☎ 92.43.23.31).

Pont du Fossé (south). Maison de la Vallée, 05260 Chabottes (☎ 92.55.73.86).

La Chapelle-en-Valgaudemar (southwest). Asile St-Paul, 05800 St-Firmin (☎ 92.55.25.19).

Vallouise (east). Maison du Parc, 05290 Vallouise (☎ 92.23.32.31).

There are minor information centres at Le Casset, Galerie, Réallon, Fressinières, Merlette and Col du Lautaret.

Glaciers/lakes. The glacial region in the centre comprises 10,000 ha. The main glaciers are Blanc, Noir, Dames du Mont de Lans and Monêtier. The mountain lakes are Lauvitel, La Muzelle, Palluel, Faravel and Lauzon. The views from the Glacier Blanc and Serre Chevalier (reached by cable car from the N91) are superb.

FAUNA

Determined efforts are being made to protect the ibex, but chamois, marmots, fox, stoat and mountain hare are more common. Red frogs and salamanders are among 30 species of reptile noted. The wild birdlife is more extensive with 110 species including the golden eagle, alpine ptarmigan, rock partridge, capercaillie, black woodpecker and Tengmalm owl. There are numerous insects including the rare butterfly Graelsie Isabella, which has four 'eyes'. The numerous rivers contain freshwater fish, especially trout.

FLORA AND VEGETATION

There are 2000 species noted which include lady's slipper orchids, orange lily, crocus, martagon lily, blue thistle (*reine des Alpes*), alpine gentian and saxifrage, *sabot de Vénus*, alpine poppies and glacial buttercups. Although the woodland, mainly larch, beech, pine and fir, covers only 5 per cent of the park, the valleys are thick with rhododendrons and dwarf juniper, as well as the rich pastureland for the alpine *moutons*.

WHAT TO DO

Walks. Walking is a major activity with 34 mountain *refuges* in case of need, including one at Merlette. The Grande Randonnée 50 comes into the park from the northwest near Le Bourg d'Oisans and continues along the northern boundary to La Grave and Col du Lautaret towards Briançon. It continues south down the eastern boundary and links with the GR 54 at Vallouise. The GR 50 keeps south to Orcières, but the GR 54 heads westwards across the centre of the park along the valley of the river Séveraisse. Then it continues due northwest through the mountains and glaciers towards Vizille and the N91. In the southwest corner appear the GR 94 and GR 93. There is a whole network of signed walks to explore. Good start points include Vallouise, La Grave, Serre-Chevalier, Briançon, La Chapelle-en-Valgaudemar, Allefroide, St-Christophe and Entraigues. Details from Park HQ and tourist offices.

Archery. *Tir à l'arc* at Les Deux-Alpes and Orcières-Merlette.

Canoe/kayak. These can be hired along the rivers Gyr, Onde, Gyronde, Drac, Guisanne and Séveraisse.

Cycling/VTT. Cycles can be rented at St-Bonnet and Le Bourg-d'Oisans. Mountain bikes can be hired at Champsaur and Clarée and in the Nevache valley. Consult Park HQ or tourist offices.

Horse-riding. There are *centres équestres* at Orcières, Vénosc, Ville-neuve-la-Salle, Le Bourg d'Oisans, Auris, Puy-St-Vincent, Vallouise, St-Michel-en-Calliol and Chazelet/La Grave.

Courses. *Stages* of two to three days are available, usually in July–Aug., in ornithology, botany, geology, fauna and local crafts. Details from tourist offices.

Skiing. Centres and ski-lifts at Les Deux-Alpes, La Grave, Puy-St-Vincent and Merlette-Orcières.

WHAT TO SEE

Natural sights. Gorges, canyons and cols along the N91 between Vizille and Briançon and the N94 south to Guillestre.

Local fêtes are held in July–Aug. in Briançon, St-Cristophe-en-Oisans, La Grave, Serre-Chevalier, Ailefroide and many other places, such as Vigneux, Vallouise, Puy-St-Vincent and Eychaude. Folklore days are held also in July–Aug. in Prapic, Orcières and Serre-Heyraud.

Churches. Worth visiting among others are those at Vallouise-la-Grave, Monêtier, St-Maurice-en-Valgaudemar and Guillestre.

Châteaux. At Glaizil, St-Jean-St-Nicolas, Vizille, Sechilienne.

Interesting village architecture. Archivard, Audiberts, Les Estaris, Prapic, Les Ratiers, Serre-Heyraud, Les Tourrengs, Les Veyers, Le Chazelet and Courtil.

Museums. In the towns of Briançon, Gap and Grenoble.

WHERE TO STAY

There are 34 *refuges de haute montagne* which offer basic lodging (total 1500 beds) for alpinists and walkers: check beforehand with Park HQ or tourist offices for reservations. There are youth hostels at Les Tourrengs near Orcières and Bez near Serre-Chevalier. Campsites are at Bourg d'Oisans (8), La Garde-en-Oisans, Serre-Chevalier (4), Vallouise (20), Villar-d'Arène, Ailefroide, La Chapelle-en-Valgaudemar (3), Chauffayer, Gaizil, St-Firmin, St-Maurice-en-Valgaudemar, Orcières, St-Michel-de-Chaillol and Chabottes. 11 communes around the park offer bed and breakfast in private houses: ask tourist offices for brochure *Gîtes Ruraux* for Isère or Hautes-Alpes. There are small hotels in most of the villages on the perimeter of the park, including St-Antoine, Pelroux, Puy-St-Vincent, La Freissinières, St-Maurice-en-Valgaudemar and Embrun.

TOURIST OFFICES

Gap. 15 rue Faure du Serre (☎ 92.51.57.03); 6 rue Silos (☎ 92.51.22.12).

Grenoble. CI Montagnes et Sentiers (☎ 76.54.34.36).

Briançon. BP 48, Porte de Pignerol (☎ 92.21.08.50); Central Parc (☎ 92.21.08.21).

Embrun. BP 49, pl. Gén.-Dosse (☎ 92.43.01.80).

Guillestre. Pl. Salva (☎ 92.45.04.37).

QUEYRAS

Region: DAUPHINÉ ALPS

Tucked away in a forgotten corner of the Hautes-Alpes, the Parc Naturel Régional du Queyras is a small Ruritanian region of unspoilt delight. The eastern border is the Italian frontier; the southern border is the valley of the river Ubaye between a dozen *pics*, *têtes* and *monts* well over 3000 m in height. The western border includes the nature reserve of Val d'Escreins and the valley of the wild river Durance which flows a long way further south into the Rhône. The northern border cuts across a mountain range south of Briançon, via the Col d'Izard back to the Italian border. Tucked away in this green mountainous park are eight communes and 2300 inhabitants. The region is rich in lakes, waterfalls and mountain springs. Founded in 1977, this Cinderella park is not only difficult to find but difficult to enter, since some of the passes are often closed by snow. The small villages of Guillestre (just outside the park), St-Véran, Aiguilles and Château-Queyras will give you a warm welcome. St-Véran claims to be the highest village in Europe. There are ski resorts, good walks, alpine fauna and flora, interesting craftspeople, photogenic peaks and the makings of an unspoilt, back-to-nature, inexpensive holiday. The key road within the park is the D902 from Guillestre, which follows the river Guil northeast to Château-Queyras, where the D902 forks north towards Briançon, and the D947 and river Guil continue northeast to Aiguilles and Abriès almost to the Italian frontier. So remote is this little mountain enclave that between 1343 and 1789 it was called the *République des Escartons*, an independent state.

Maps. Michelin 77; IGN 54, 244–6.

Access. From Briançon southeast by D902 or south to Mont-Dauphin and Guillestre by N94. From Gap northeast by N94 through Savines and Embrun. SNCF to Briançon, Gap and Mont-Dauphin. Buses from Briançon or Guillestre into the park.

Park HQ. Maison du Parc, rte de la Gare, BP 3, 05600 Guillestre (☎ 92.45.06.23) and other information points in the centre of the park:

Maison du Queyras, 05470 Aiguilles (☎ 92.45.76.18); Maison du Roy on D947; and, in summer only, at the Col de l'Izoard on D902.

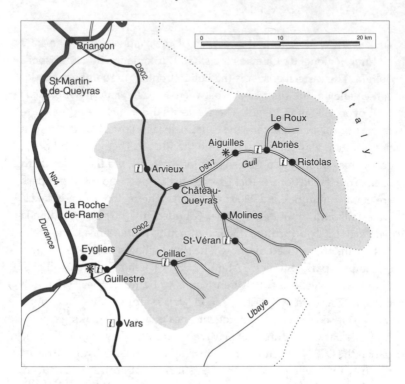

FAUNA

Chamois abound on the mountainsides, as do mountain hare and, lower down, marmot and fox. One of the best places to see chamois is in the reserve of the valley of Ségure near the Lac d'Egorgéou close to the Italian frontier. The Park HQ is now encouraging stag, deer and wild sheep (*mouflon*). Among 80 species of bird are the golden and royal eagles, falcons, ptarmigan (*lagopède des Alpes*), Bartavelle partridge, spotted nuthatch, owls, woodpeckers and capercaillie (*grand tétras*). The eagles regard marmot as tasty prey. Among the silver pines are the rare Isabella butterfly and the Spanish moon moth. The mountain lakes and half dozen rivers all have freshwater fish including trout. Thousands of sheep take part in the transhumance to and from the mountain pastures.

PNR Volcans d'Auvergne – Top: *Gentiana verna* (photo P. Rozier)
PNR Mercantour – Below: Mouflon, wild sheep (photo G. Lombart)

PNR Mercantour – Left: A hare in its winter coat   Right: Ermine
(photos G. Lombart)

PRN Mercantour – Left: Golden Eagle   Right: Ptarmigan (photos G. Lombart)

PNR Mercantour – Left: Marmot (photo G. Lombart)
Right: Fox (photo R. Settimo)

FLORA AND VEGETATION

The park is rich in mountain and sub-alpine vegetation with up to 2000 species of plant. The forests are mainly larch, spruce, pine and fir. Forty species of flower are protected within the park, including edelweiss, arnica, camomile, gentian, angelica, orchid, ranunculus, violet and forget-me-not, and a rarity deriving from the Caucasus, foxtail vetch. Around St-Véran you will see most of these flowers, also juniper, which makes an agreeable local liqueur. The nature reserve of Val d'Escreins near Vars in the southwest corner, open 15 June–30 Sept., has botanical trails to see the mountain and sub-alpine flora. Contact the Office de Tourisme, cours Fontana Rosa, Vars (☎ 92.46.51.31).

WHAT TO DO

Walks. The Grande Randonnée 5 leads southeast from Briançon south of Col d'Izouard to Château-Queyras, then south to Ceillac, Lac Ste-Anne and over the Pic de la Pont Sancte. The GR 541 enters the park from the west at St-Crépin, which is north of Mont-Dauphin, and goes southeast through the Val d'Escreins. The GR 58 starts in the southeast corner of the park on the Italian border at Le Pain de Sucre, heads west to St-Véran, runs west of Château-Queyras and up the valley of the Rivière, and follows the mountain ridges northeast to the Grand Vallon and to Pic du Malrif, where it spawns four offshoots, GR 58A, B, C and D. The GR 58 doubles back and appears near the Lac Egourgéou not far from the Italian border in the southeast corner of the park.

Local walks are organised in the Haut-Queyras from St-Véran (☎ 92.45.81.33); in the Viso from Abriès (☎ 92.45.75.66); in Queyras from Arvieux (☎ 92.46.73.86); and from Autrans (☎ 92.95.33.25).

For photographic ornithological *randonnées* from Abriès ☎ 92.45.73.54.

Climbing. For *escalades* and *alpinisme* there are mountain guides at Ceillac (☎ 92.45.05.74); at Molines (☎ 92.45.84.13); and Queyras-Viso, Abriès (☎ 92.45.72.26).

Cycling/VTT. Cycles can be rented at Aiguilles or Château-Queyras.

Horse-riding. *Centres équestres* at Eygliers and Vars.

Canoe/kayak. Down the river Guil from Ristolas or Abriès or less strenuously on the man-made *plan d'eau* at Eygliers.

Fishing. Trout fishing is possible in any of 11 mountain lakes. Permits from Aiguilles or Guillestre.

Skiing. Fairly recently the park authorities have developed winter ski facilities and now there are 130 km of *pistes* and a further 250 km of cross-country runs. There are 10 ski schools with 42 ski-lifts, mainly round Abriès, Ristolas and Le Roux in the northeast corner of the park. Information from Maisons du Parc and tourist offices.

Courses. A variety of *stages* are organised at Guillestre and Peyre-Belle.

WHAT TO SEE

Château-Queyras, fortified by Vauban for Louis XIV, was the former capital of the République des Escartons founded in 1343. In the summer it is floodlit at night.

16thC churches at Ceillac and Abriès and mountain chapels at Marbre (Notre-Dame-de-Clausis), Eygliers, Molines, Arvieux and a dozen other places on the GR trails.

Crafts. Carved wood objects including toys, music-boxes and puzzles, pottery, knitware, leatherware and wickerwork are made by craftspeople all over the park, plus cheeses and honey. Consult the Syndicat des Artisans d'Art, Maison du Queyras, Aiguilles (☎ 92.45.75.06).

Fêtes/foires. Molines (Fête St-Simon), Aiguilles, Ceillac and Guillestre all have *fêtes* during the summer.

PHOTOGENIC NATURAL SIGHTS

Tête Noire peak (3175 m) at the end of the Aigue Blanche river, reached by GR 58 from St-Véran. Flora and fauna at their best.

Lac de Ste-Anne on the GR 5 southeast of Ceillac, once the site of a pagan cult, and then a pilgrimage route to the little chapel of Ste-Anne on 26 July.

Belvédère de Mont Viso (2127 m) on the GR 58C looks across the Italian frontier at the 3841 m high lake of Viso.

Lac Foréant. Large glacial lakes at 2608 m on the GR 58 and the Queyras trail via 13 *gîtes d'étape*. Close to Lac Egourgéou.

Vallée du Guil (1600 m) at the end of the D947 up the river valley of Guin below the ski centres, *pics, crîtes* and *têtes* reached by GR 58 and 58D.

La Casse Déserte and *Col d'Izoard* where the D902 struggles and wriggles its way past the Refuge Napoléon on the way to Briançon. The highest point of the Tour de France, ridden by international cyclists in midsummer.

WHERE TO STAY

For walkers there are *gîtes d'étape* and *refuges* in 13 places. Ask Park HQ for map. There are five youth hostels at Guillestre, Vars, Ceillac, St-Véran and Chaux, and 18 campsites of which seven are near Guillestre. Hotels and *auberges* are in Ristolas, Guillestre, Vars, St-Véran, Abriès and Arvieux. Ask tourist offices for details.

TOURIST OFFICES

Guillestre (☎ 92.45.04.37). Ceillac (☎ 92.45.75.76). Arvieux (☎ 92.45.05.74). Vars (☎ 92.45.51.31). Abriès (☎ 92.45.72.26). St-Véran (☎ 92.45.82.21. Ristolas (☎ 92.45.72.26).

MERCANTOUR

Region: FRENCH ALPS

Inland from Nice and Menton on the Côte d'Azur lies one of the major national parks – a superb blend of mountains, rich flora and fauna, top-class winter skiing and some remarkable Bronze Age rock engravings. The Mercantour national park was created in 1979, is long and narrow in shape and follows the frontier with Italy. It occupies 68,500 ha, mainly in the Alpes-Maritime *département* but with a quarter in the Alpes-de-Haute-Provence. It is twinned with the Canadian park of Banff in the Rocky Mountains. There are two zones. The central zone, from Col de Larche in the north to Col de Brouis in the south, is nearly 80 km in length and about 10 km wide, except at the southern and northern ends. For 30 km it adjoins the Italian national park of Argentera with game such as *bouquetin* (ibex) crossing the frontier at will. The outer zone, which contains 28 communes with a population of 18,000, extends around the foothills of five main valleys. From north to south these are those of the rivers Ubaye, Hautvar et Hautverdon, Tinée, Vésubie and Roya. Among the principal villages are Jausiers, Colmars, Allos, St-Étienne-de-Tinée, St-Martin-Vésubie, Valdeblore, Peira-Cava, Turini, Tende and St-Dalmas-de-Tende.

Several rivers which rise in the mountains, such as the Tinée and Vésubie, flow southwest to join the Var, which enters the Mediterranean near Nice airport. But the rugged granite and glacial mountains dominate the park: Mont Pelat (3051 m), Tête de l'Enchastraye (2995 m), Mont Ténibre (3031 m), Mont Mounier (2817 m) and Mont Bégo (2873 m). There are a number of large lakes at high altitudes: Lacs d'Allos, Vens and Rabuons, and further southeast half a dozen around the Vallée des Merveilles. The mountain walks are challenging but 600 km of trails are marked, including several Grandes Randonnées. The three well-known ski resorts of Isola 2000, Auron and Valberg are in the northwest sector of the park, reached by D28/D2205. Of 4200 flower species known in France, 2000 can be found in the park, and 40 are found only in the Mercantour. Perhaps surprisingly animal life is abundant, and avifauna and insects, more predictably, are as interesting as in any other nature park. Alpine plants and rhododendrons grow on the heights and a wide variety of trees on the slopes.

Maps. Michelin 81, 84; IGN 61.

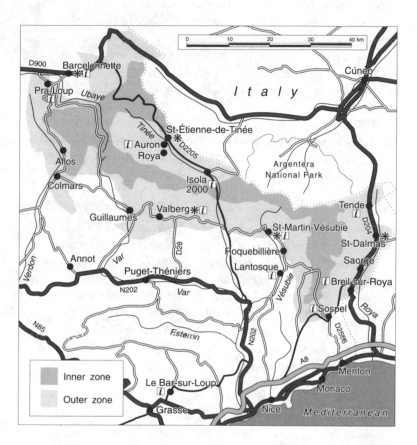

Access. By car from Menton on the D2566, a winding road north to Sospel to the N204 and Tende on the eastern boundary of the park, by car from Nice north on the N202 and D2565 to St-Martin-Vésubie. From Digne northeast by D900 to Barcelonnette. From Gap east on the N94 to Savines, D954 and D900 to Barcelonnette. Buses go from the *gares routières* in Nice and Menton. Train from Nice-Coni to Sospel, Breil-sur-Roya, Saorge, St-Dalmas and Tende.

Park HQ. The administrative HQ is at 23 rue d'Italie, 06000 Nice (☎ 93.87.86.10) – at least 30 km away from the park. Ask for their leaflet

Haut Pays de la Côte d'Azur et Parc National du Mercantour. There is also a basic Maison du Parc in each of the valleys:

La Sapinière, 04400 Barcelonnette (☎ 92.81.21.31) on D900, northwest corner.

Quartier de l'Ardon, 06660 St-Étienne-de-Tinée (☎ 93.02.42.27) on D2205 northwest of Isola.

Maison Valberganne, 06470 Valberg (☎ 93.02.58.23) on D28 east of Guillaumes.

PNM, pl. de la Mairie, 06450 St-Martin-Vésubie (☎ 93.03.23.15) on D2565 northwest of Lantosque.

PNM, La Minière, 06430 St-Dalmas-de-Tende (☎ 93.04.67.00) on N204 between Tende and Saorge.

FAUNA

The three prolific species are 3000 mountain chamois, ibex (*bouquetin*) reintroduced from the Italian side, and about 300 of the Corsican wild sheep (*mouflon*). Other species include alpine hare, fox, stoat (brown in summer, white in winter), marmot and wildcat (*civet*). Birds of prey (*rapaces*) include the royal eagle, golden eagle, eagle owl, buzzard, sparrowhawk, kite and harrier. Also seen are blackcock (*tétras*), ptarmigan (known as snow partridge) and Tengmalm owl. Insects include the larche ringlet, and there are also small apollo butterflies. Be careful of adders near the lakes.

FLORA AND VEGETATION

From 700 m to 2500 m one finds a wide variety of trees, reflecting the blend of Mediterranean and alpine climates which encourage oak, olive, fir, pine, spruce and larch. Above 2500 m are clumps of rhododendron and alpine flowers. Saxifrage with its spiky, rose-coloured flowers, blue spring gentian, houseleek and orchids can be seen, as well as the St Bruno lily, digitalis, yellow and violet pansies, wood geraniums, St Antony oleander, pinks and chiron centaury. *Saxifraga florulenta* has been adopted as the park's symbol.

WHAT TO DO

Walks. The park has a complex network of marked trails. Three Grandes Randonnées cross it on a north–south axis, and two cross roughly east–west and parallel to each other. The 600 km of signed walks have no fewer than 45 hostels and relay-stations with between 8 and 80 beds plus restaurant or cooking facilities. The GR 4 starts at Grasse north-west of Cannes and eventually reaches the Gorges de Verdon. The GR 5 from Nice heading for Amsterdam enters the park near Roure, continues northwest near Mont Mounier, Roya, Auron, St-Étienne-de-Tinée and Bousieyas, and exits at Col de Larche in the northwest corner. The GR 52 starts at Menton, heads north through Sospel across the Turini range and Vallée des Merveilles, then west alongside the river Vionene, and turns southwards out of the park to Valdeblore.

The east–west axis trails are the GR 52A from Tende to Col des Champs, and GR 51A, called *Sentier des Huit Vallées*, from the Italian frontier to St-Cézaire using old walks crossing the valleys of the Roya, Bévera, Vésubie, Tinée, Cians, Var, Esteron and Siagne. This is the least-known and most interesting GR. Ask the tourist or park offices for a copy of *Alpes-Maritimes Randonnées*. Information can also be obtained from CIMES-GTA, 7 rue Voltaire, 38000 Grenoble. The Bureau des Guides, 51 rue Cotta, 06430 Tende (☎ 93.04.68.72) has a roster of experienced guides for hire.

Climbing. The best season for *escalade-alpinisme* is June–Oct. A wide range of climbs is available from 'difficult', e.g. crossing the mountain ridges of St-Robert-au-Gelas, to 'very difficult', e.g. the Yellow Face at Cougourde. The Club Alpin Français (CAF) offers climbing courses in the park at St-Dalmas-de-Valdeblore, Le Boréon, Roquebillière, Belvédère, Valberg, St-Étienne-de-Tinée, Auron, Isola 2000 and Tende. Consult CAF at Barcelonnette (☎ 92.81.04.73).

Caving. Courses in potholing (*spéléologie*) take place in July–Aug. in the massif of Marguareis. Consult the Bureau des Guides de Tende (see above).

Horse-riding. There are four small *centres équestres* at Roya (☎ 93.92.42.12); Auron (☎ 93.23.00.72); Barcelonnette (☎ 92.81.25.78); and Pra-Loup (☎ 92.84.10.04).

Hang-gliding. Courses are organised at St-Dalmas-de-Valdeblore (☎ 93.02.83.50), May–Dec.; and at Pra-Loup (☎ 92.84.18.72). Information from Fédération Française de Vol Libre, 54bis rue de la Buffa, 06000 Nice (☎ 93.88.62.89).

Canoe/kayak. This popular sport can be practised on the rivers Var (5 descents), Tinée (4 descents), Vésubie (5 descents) and Roya (3 descents). Of these the Roya is the ideal river. Information from Association Plein Air Nature (Kayak), 14 bd Hugo, 04000 Digne (☎ 92.31.51.09).

Cycling/VTT. Cycle hire at Isola 2000, Auron, Valberg, Barcelonnette and Allos. Information from tourist offices.

Skiing. There are three international resorts at Auron, Isola 2000 and Valberg, two medium-sized ones at La Colmiane-Valdeblore and Greolières-les-Neiges, and 12 mountain village resorts. Information from Ski-Azur CRT, 55 promenade des Anglais, 06000 Nice. Altogether there are 250 ski trails, 600 km in length, 155 ski-lifts and every permutation – alpine, cross-country, ski jumping, slalom, etc.

Fishing. There is ample opportunity to fish in all the rivers, but a permit is needed. Consult the tourist offices.

Alpes d'Azur. In collaboration with IBM a special computer program has been devised which produces every possible item of tourist information. Based in the commercial centre of CAP 3000 near Nice, there are no less than sixteen sites in the *zone périphérique* of the park. Ask any tourist office for the programme 'ALPES d'AZUR' on their *micro-ordinateur*.

WHAT TO SEE

La Vallée des Merveilles is a unique site halfway between St-Martin-Vésubie and Tende, reached on foot by GR 52 with two *refuges* at Lac Long and Lac Vert. 100,000 rock drawings (*rupestres*) produced by Bronze Age man 4000 years ago are one of the wonders of the world, visited by hundreds of thousands of walkers each year. There are two minor trails to the spot – *sentier Bicknell* and *la voie Fontnalba*. The usual 20thC problems occur of theft, vandalism and graffiti, despite almost constant surveillance.

Lac d'Allos (50 ha), at a height of 2729 m, is visited by 20,000 walkers each year and is reached by the D226 east of Allos. The Park HQ has recently placed 13 different information tables around the 2 km lake circuit. Parking 40 minutes walk from the lake. There are pastures nearby for transhumance sheep visits.

Le Boréon in the centre of the park on the D89 is the departure point for several walks and has 1500 chamois and 300 *mouflons* wild on the slopes.

Le Col de la Cayolle at 2317 m on the D2202 between Entraunes and Pra-Loup. Walk in the alpine garden in the hamlet of Estenc where the river Var rises. There are numerous marmots on view.

L'Authion at 1900 m west of Saorges. A military fortress with superb views of Corsica, the Mediterranean and the region of the Merveilles and La Roya.

La Madone de Fenestra at 1900 m on the old Route du Sel and a pilgrimage site with summer processions. Several trails start here, reached by the D94 northeast from St-Martin-Vésubie.

Le Col de la Bonette at 2802 m is a major sheep transhumance centre and well-known beauty spot on the D64.

WHERE TO STAY

There are 38 campsites in the foothills around the park, seven youth hostels, many *gîtes d'étape*, 45 mountain *refuges* accessible only on foot, and a wide range of hotels in the ski resorts and *auberges* in the mountain villages. Maisons du Parc and/or tourist offices have lists and may make reservations on your behalf. In midsummer reservations are essential.

Village bases. Apart from the smart ski-resorts there are half a dozen small towns or villages with hotels and restaurants, which make ideal bases for a Mercantour Park holiday. From NW to SE Guillaumes (pop. 546), see Queen Jeanne's castle, the parade of the Empire Artillerymen on 15 August, and listen to medieval music concerts. Valberg (pop.

635), sledge dog racing (Jan.), world championship of Winter Triathlons (March), Feast of 'Our Lady of the Snows' (August). St Martin-Vesubie (pop. 1156), geographic 'centre' of the park; rambling, trout fishing, rock climbing, good skiing. Patron saints days in August and Sept. Sospel (pop. 2278), see the cathedral, Holy Cross chapel and 'Maginot Line' fortifications. Music and painting festivals. Marathon race to Turini in Oct. Breil-sur-Roya (pop. 2159), handy for visits to the Saorge, Agnon and Brouis gorges and valleys, tour of the lakes, Valley of the Marvels. The old town has medieval towers, churches, chapels, a monastery, and holds many festivals. Tende (pop. 2045). Good base for visiting Valley of the Marvels. Best centre for festivals (spring fair, mule cavalcade to St Eligius, two saint's feast days (Lady of Vievola in July, Ste Anne de Granile in August). Shepherds' festival, folklore festival, chestnut festival in the old town, autumn fairs.

TOURIST OFFICES

Auron (☎ 93.23.02.66). Isola 2000 (☎ 93.23.15.15). Ubaye (☎ 92.84.10.04). Valberg (☎ 93.02.52.77). Pra-Loup (☎ 92.84.10.04). La Colmiane-Valdeblore (☎ 93.02.84.59). Tende (☎ 93.04.62.64). Breil-sur-Roya (☎ 93.04.41.29). Lantosque (☎ 93.03.00.02). Le Bar-sur-Loup (☎ 93.42.72.21). St-Martin-Vésubie (☎ 93.03.21.28). Sospel (☎ 93.04.00.19). Barcelonnette (☎ 92.81.04.71).

LUBÉRON

Region: PROVENCE

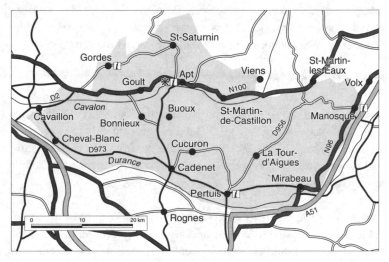

Created in 1977, the Parc Naturel du Lubéron consists of 130,000 ha spread over 57 communes with 85,000 inhabitants in the *départements* of Vaucluse and Alpes-de-Haut Provence. The river Durance and the D973 form the southern boundary. After Mirabeau the river widens and the valley runs due north to Manosque, parallel to the N96 and A51. The northern boundary is the N100 which runs through Apt almost to the outskirts of Cavaillon in the west. The mountain range of Lubéron runs for 70 km west–east with modest peaks up to 1100 m, ideal for walkers. Most of the park is either forested or farmed and presents an attractive rural landscape with lavender beds, fruit trees, vines, olives and cereals. The region is well known for its excellent flora, caves, steep-sided valleys and *villages perchés*. With a Mediterranean climate the *maquis* and *garrigue* flourish in a tangle of aromatic shrubs and herbs. The towns of significance are Apt (pop. 11,600) in the centre-north, famous for its crystallised fruit, Manosque (pop. 19,600) on the eastern side and Pertuis (pop. 12,500) on the southern border. Cadenet (pop. 2640), Bonnieux (pop. 1500) and Ménerbes (pop. 1000) are villages in the centre of the park. The river Durance, which flows eventually into the Rhône, is fed by fast-flowing streams. The river Calavon joins the Coulon near Cavaillon and links with the Durance on the western border. A multitude of minor roads within the park makes travel easy. There are several interesting abbeys, châteaux and museums to see. Also in the countryside the round medieval stone refuges called *les bories* can be seen from the Grandes Randonnées walks. The best time to visit is in the spring or at vintage time in October to taste the young wines of the Côtes de Lubéron.

Maps. Michelin 81, 84; IGN 60, 67, 68.

Access. From Aix-en-Provence northwards by A51, N96 or D556. From Cavaillon eastwards by D2 or D973. From Forcalquier in the northeast southwards by N100 or D13. SNCF routes go from Aix to Manosque and from Cavaillon to Pertuis. Many buses operate out of Apt, Cavaillon and Manosque.

Park HQ. 1 pl. Jean-Jaurès, 84400 Apt (☎ 90.74.08.55). It has a museum, exhibitions, the usual literature, and also tasting/buying facilities for local wines, foods and craft work. Another source of park information is to be found at the Château de la Tour d'Aigues (☎ 90.77.50.33) also with a museum and wine-tasting facilities, on the D956 6 km northeast of Pertuis. The third information point is in the Fort de Buoux (☎ 90.74.08.55), just east of Bonnieux on the D113.

FAUNA

European beaver and otter survive in the Durance and Calavon rivers, and wild boar, fox, stone marten, weasel and badger on the hill slopes among the *garrigue*. Sheep graze hopefully on the sun-dried fields and goats provide *fromage de chèvre*. There are 130 species of nesting bird which inhabit the rocky limestone cliffs, including eagle (Bonelli and Jean-le-Blanc), Egyptian vulture, kestrels, falcons, buzzards and the timid Grand-Duc owl, which all feed on the lizards, salamanders and grass-snakes. Other varieties include the blue rock thrush and alpine swift, nightingale and hoopoe. The small river Aiguebrun has recently been cleared and cleaned, and freshwater fish will thrive.

FLORA AND VEGETATION

The *maquis* vegetation is dominated by holm oak (*ilex*), mainly coppiced oak forests and 1000 ha of Atlas cedar planted in 1860 on the ridge of the Petit Lubéron on the forest road from Bonnieux to Cheval-Blanc. The forest of Pélicier near St-Martin-les-Eaux in the northeast corner consists of Austrian black pine trees originally grown here in the 19thC. In the spring rock rose, orchids, grape hyacinths, wild pinks, jonquils, mauve, blue and purple iris, pink valerian, buttercups and jasmine, even yellow tulips, flourish among the juniper and thyme. The park authorities are particularly proud of the yellow Villars *gênet* found in the top mountain craters, aspic lavender, Montpellier maple, rose-violet coloured *ciste cotonneux* and *leuzée à cone*. This is butterfly countryside – adonis blues, swallowtails, clouded yellows and many other varieties can be seen. In the valleys are orchards of cherries, peaches and pears trained on cordons, espaliers and double espaliers.

WHAT TO DO

Walks. The Park HQ has prepared a topoguide *20 Promenades et Randonnées dans le Parc*. In particular it recommends a 2 hour botanical walk in the cedar forest of Petit Lubéron, a 1 hour walk from the village of Roussillon to see the amazing ochre-coloured sandstone outcrops, a 3 hour walk to see the *bories* at Viens and a 2 hour walk to see the restored amphitheatre and terraces at Goult. The Grande Randonnée 9 comes in to the park north of Apt, crosses the Grand Lubéron range, turns east, then south and exits at Mirabeau. The GR 4 comes in from the east at Manosque and becomes the 4-97 and heads north to Oppedette. Permutations of the GR 9 (e.g 97, 9-97) head towards Cavaillon along the central mountain range. The 6-97 covers the northern and western boundaries. Around the highest peak, Mourre Nègre southeast of Apt, are the GR 9-97, 92 and 97.

Horse-riding. *Centres équestres* are at Apt (Relais de Roquefurez and Cheval en Lubéron), Roussillon, Goult, Maubec, Bonnieux, Cucuron, Castellet, Viens, St-Martin-de-la-Brasouis and Cheval-Blanc.

Cycling/VTT. This is a popular activity and the Park HQ recommends Apt-Cavaillon (40 km by minor roads) and Apt-St-Martin-de-Castillon

(15 km by country tracks). Cycle rental at Cadenet, Bonnieux, Tour-d'Aigues and Cucuron. Details from Park HQ.

Borie visits. The three main areas are around Gordes and Sénanque abbey (northwest), on the Claparèdes plateau near Bonnieux and Buoux (centre) and on the Caseneuve plateau near Viens and St-Martin-de-Castillon (east of Apt).

Canoe/kayak. Facilities for rental exist along the Durance river at Manosque, Pertuis and Cadenet.

Fishing. Trout fishing is available in park rivers, but a permit is required.

WHAT TO SEE

Museums

At *Apt* the Maison du Parc has a museum of palaeonthology.

Château de la Tour d'Aigues, northeast of Pertuis, has the Musée de l'Oeuvre containing ceramics; also Musée de l'Histoire du Pays d'Aigues.

Lourmarin has the Musée Philippe de Girard and Musée du Château.

Gordes has the Musée Vasarély in the château and nearby Musée du Vitrail (stained glass).

At *Ansouis* is the Musée des Poissons du Lubéron and Musée du Château.

Bonnieux has the Musée de la Boulangerie; *Cucuron* an archaeological museum; *Oppède-le-Vieux* a mineral and fossil museum; *Montfuron* has a geological museum called the Musée Jean Fabre; *Manosque* has a municipal museum.

Châteaux. La Tour d'Aigues, Lourmarin, the Fort du Buoux, Ansouis, Cucuron and Gordes are all worth seeing. Lacost château was once owned by the notorious Marquis de Sade.

Abbeys/churches. The Abbaye de Sénanque (northwest of Gordes) has two small museums and is outstanding; so too are the Abbaye de Silvacane (south of Cadenet) and the Basilique de Ste Anne in Apt. At

Carluc off the N100 east of Apt is the religious complex of monastery, priory and churches.

Town visits. Roussillon for its ochre splendours, known as Colorado Provençal; Gordes for its spectacular hillside view and château-museum; Oppède-le-Vieux is a *village perché* with a craft colony; Apt's *vieille ville*, cathedral and museums should be seen.

Observatories. St-Michel and Haute-Provence observatories southwest of Forcalquier.

WHERE TO STAY

There are scores of campsites, *gîtes ruraux, relais d'étapes* (for walkers and riders) and *chambres d'hôte*. Ask for details from tourist offices. Modest hotels are available in Apt, Pertuis, Manosque and Cadenet, but are more expensive at Gordes.

TOURIST OFFICES

Apt. 2 ave. Philippe-Girard (☎ 90.74.03.18).
Pertuis. Tour du Clocher, pl. Mirabeau (☎ 90.79.15.56).
Gordes. Pl. du Château (☎ 90.72.02.75).
Manosque. Pl. Dr P. Joubert (☎ 92.72.16.00).

REGIONAL VISITS

Northwest on the far side of the river Durance, centred round Digne, is the Réserve Géologique de Haut-Provence.

The Vaucluse Fountain west of Gordes is the spectacular source of the river Sorgue, made famous by Petrarch's love poems.

The wine regions of Côtes de Lubéron, Côtes de Ventoux and Côtes d'Aix all lie within one hour's drive of the park.

The Montagne de Ste Victoire and Aix-en-Provence are to the south.

PORT-CROS

Region: CÔTE D'AZUR

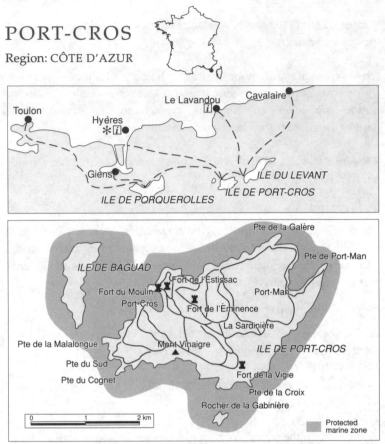

Fifteen kilometres of Mediterranean Sea separate this national park from Hyères on the Côte d'Azur mainland. The park, which falls within the Var *département*, is distinctive because more than half its area is under water (*sous-marin*) forming a marine zone around the island of Port-Cros which protects a Mediterranean underwater forest. Created in 1963, the island park of Port-Cros is 4 km long by 2.4 km in width, and with 650 ha above water it is the smallest of France's nature parks. In the centre of the Iles d'Hyères, the park does not include the well-known Ile de Porquerolles to the west, nor the Ile du Levant to the east. But it does include three little neighbouring islets – Bagaud (40 ha), La Gabinière and Rascas – as well as a marine zone of 600 metres around the island, which make a grand total of 1800 ha. The island is hilly with Mont Vinaigre reaching 194 m and is densely covered in forest. Mammals are uninteresting, but bird, insect and fish species thrive in a heavily protected ambience: the human population is only about 30, mainly consisting of fishermen. There are 35 km of marked walks radiating out from the small port of Port-Cros, and there are 18 old forts and batteries as the island was a defence against sea-borne marauders, including the British Navy in the Napoleonic Wars. The views from the dozen *pointes* and *caps* are superlative. Access is relatively easy, but accommodation is very limited. Nevertheless a day visit is extremely rewarding. From June–Sept. there is an underwater trail, using flippers and snorkel, to look at the Mediterranean botany.

Maps. Michelin 84; IGN 67, 68.

Access. Only by ship (between 45 and 75 minutes) from Hyères, Le Lavandou and La Tour Fondue at Presqu'île de Giens, south of Hyères. During summer, sailings are hourly. From Hyères, Transport Littoral Varois (TLV), Port St-Pierre (☎ 94.57.44.07); from Le Lavandou, Cie Vildor, 15 quai Gabriel-Péri (☎ 94.71.01.02); and from Giens, Cie TLV, Port de la Tour Fondue (☎ 94.58.21.81). Access to Hyères by air, train or bus.

Park HQ. Parc National de Port-Cros, Castel Ste-Claire, rue Ste-Claire, 83400 Hyères (☎ 94.65.32.98). On the island there is an information centre in the port (☎ 94.05.90.17).

FAUNA

A black rat-like squirrel, rabbits, fieldmice, six species of snake, several lizards, gecko and a unique Tyrrhenian painted frog can be seen among the heavily wooded hills. As the island lies on a migration route birdlife is varied. In April birds in passage from Africa flit through the foliage – blackcap, willow and wood warbler, pied flycatcher and hoopoe. Breeding birds include falcon, blue blackbird, swift, Cory's shearwater and Manx shearwater. Around the rocky cliffs one can see silver seagulls, Bassan gannets, cormorants and puffins. In the woods listen to the turtledoves, nightingales and various owls. The rich insect fauna include 220 species of butterfly (among which is the two-tailed pasha) and moth, 600 species of beetle, and grasshoppers, cicadas and crickets everywhere. Among the rocks and aquatic plants offshore there live groupers, octopus, seals, eel, crayfish, lobster, crab, winkles and sea-urchins. The tiny islet of Bagaud is a nature reserve, but no access is permitted.

FLORA AND VEGETATION

Vegetation cover is dense with holm oak, Aleppo pine and also wild olive trees and bilberry. Eucalyptus and palm trees have been imported by man. Among the *maquis* scrub and heath are 1000 varieties of mushroom, and along the shoreline marine algae and blue seaweed.

WHAT TO DO

Walks. There is a circular walk from Port-Cros southwest to Pointe de la Malalongue, Pointe du Sud, Pointe du Cognet and then east over Mont Vinaigre overlooking the southern escarpment. Then inland past Fort de la Vigie, La Sardinière, Port-Man and round the northern cliffs and southwest past the forts of Estissac and Moulin back to Port Cros. The walks are often through the woods and shaded from the fierce sun.

A specific walk from the Fort de l'Estissac round the other main forts takes nearly 5 hours plus 1 hour to explore and photograph the forts. Ask for a route plan from the harbour information point.

Tours. A gentle sub-marine tour can be made, 8 m underwater, to see the fauna and flora in the bay of La Palud, round the northern corner of the main harbour. Details from the information centre.

A one-hour marine tour for groups of ten on the little ship *Terre* with glass aquascope has a commentator. Fee. Information from the tourist office.

Fort de l'Estissac. There are an aquarium, audiovisual programme, exhibitions and a small museum of sub-marine archaeological finds. Fee.

Fort de l'Éminence. This well-constructed Napoleonic fortress has been transformed by the park into dormitories and a botanic library and is, in effect, a superior youth hostel.

Beaches. There are two small beaches, Plage du Sud and Plage de la Palud, within walking distance from the port.

WHERE TO STAY

Two hotels exist – Le Manoir (☎ 94.05.90.52) and Le Provençal. There are no campsites or *gîtes* on the island, so a reservation at either hotel is essential.

TOURIST OFFICES

Hyères. Park Hotel, ave. de Belgique (☎ 94.65.18.55).
Le Lavandou. Quai Gabriel-Péri (☎ 94.71.00.61).

EXCURSIONS

Ile de Porquerolles, the largest in the Hyères group, is inhabited and cultivated. A park and botanic conservatory with hundreds of varieties of olive trees, fig trees and mulberries at La Tour-Ste-Agathe is also run by the Port-Cros national park and there are many forts, beaches, walks, cycle rides and good restaurants.

Ile du Levant is very close to the east. It is mainly occupied by the French armed services (900 ha out of 1000 ha) but visits are possible to see Fort Heliopolis and the attractive *calanques* (fiords) of Estable and Avis.

CORSICA

Region: CORSE

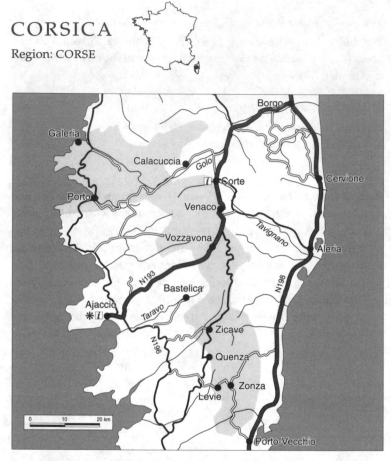

Corsica is separated from Sardinia by only 12 km of sea, is only 82 km east of Italian Tuscany and is 162 km south of Provence. This is probably the reason why the old Corsican dialect spoken in rural areas is closer to Italian than to French.

The whole island is beautiful but beset with environmental problems: forest clearance, excessive hunting, frequent fires which destroy the *maquis* vegetation, some banditry and, in midsummer, an overdose of tourism. Try to visit out of season in the spring or autumn. It is still mainly a rural economy apart from income from tourism, with livestock grazing and transhumance, when in the spring herdsmen lead their sheep and goat flocks up to the mountain pastures. There they live in traditional huts until the autumn, when they return to the lowlands.

The Parc Naturel Régional de Corse was created in May 1972 and covers almost a third of the island. The 250,000 ha also include the nature reserves of Scandola (1919 ha) and the islands of Cerbicale (36 ha) and Lavezzi (79 ha). There are 82 communities with 24,000 inhabitants within the park, spread over the two *départements* of Haute-Corse and Corse-du-Sud.

The park extends from the coastal reserve of Scandola in the west inland to include Corte, Mont Rotondo (2622 m) and Vizzavona, then in a southerly direction takes in Zicavo, Mont Incudine (2136 m) and Zonza, and ends at Porto-Vecchio on the southeast coast. There are more than 20 granite mountain peaks over 2000 m and the terrain is spectacular with bays, peninsulas, deltas, marshes and the rivers of Golo, Tavignano, Gravona and Taravo.

Maps. Michelin 90; IGN 73, 74, 116.

Access. By ship from French or Italian ports to Bastia (northeast) or Ajaccio (west coast) or frequent flights to Ajaccio-Campo dell'Oro, Bonifacio or Bastia-Poretta. Inland the main roads are N193 (Ajaccio–Bastia), N198 (the whole eastern coast) and N196 (south from Ajaccio). Local trains and buses run between Porto-Vecchio and Ajaccio, Bastia and Calvi.

Park HQ. Maison du Parc Naturel Régional de Corse, BP 417, 4 rue Général Fiorella, 20184 Ajaccio (☎ 95.21.56.54). 0830–1200, 1400–1830. Closed Sat./Sun. There are approximately 70 staff, 15 of whom are seasonal, and the majority work in the field protecting the park, particularly against fire.

There are two minor park posts at Porto (Magazinu Genovese) and Paesollo d'Aitone (between Evisa and the Col de Vergio).

FAUNA

The *mouflon* (wild sheep) and red deer, both once threatened, are now protected species. The native Corsican stag has died out, but the Sardinian variety has been introduced. Wild boar lurk in the mountains, as do stoat, red fox, rare bats, lizards, geckos, tree frogs and snakes. The streams and lakes have a variety of freshwater fish, and monk seals can be seen off the coast. The bird population is considerable. Nesting ospreys and lammergeiers are seen rarely, but along the coast are Cory's shearwater, puffins, and a wide variety of gulls including audouin. In the marshy areas and lakes purple herons, marsh harriers and moustached warblers can be seen. The wooded mountains are home to peregrine falcons, eagles, Corsican nuthatch, Corsican buzzard, alpine accentor, goshawk, red kite, bee-eater, blue rock thrush, rock sparrow, spotless starling, blue blackbirds and the Marmoras warbler. Unfortunately there is often a divide between the Corsican hunter's view of these birds and that of the ornithologist.

FLORA AND VEGETATION

Over 60 species of Mediterranean flora have been identified on the island. The Corsican pine grows to a height of 50 m and other species include Aleppo pine, silver fir, stone pine and maritime pine. Cork oak, holm oak and evergreen oak are common. In the scrub and *maquis* one finds myrtle, viburnums, strawberry trees, tree heaths, many grasses and rare algae. In the spring look out for crocus, anemones, narcissi, cyclamen and up to 50 species of orchid. The three major Larico pine forests of Aitone, Bavella and Vizzavona are among the island's main attractions.

Scandola Nature Reserve. Each year 30,000 visitors arrive on this small rock promontory on the north side of the Gulf of Porto (western side of island) to explore the caves and see the wild goats, golden eagles, ospreys and Cory's shearwaters nesting. This is one of only two French marine nature reserves, the other being Cerbères off Banyuls-sur-Mer (southeast of Perpignan).

WHAT TO DO

Walks. The Grande Randonnée 20 starts just south of Calvi and covers 150 km southeast to just north of Porto-Vecchio. A number of organisations provide guided walks for a fee along all or part of the GR 20 including Assozio Muntagnoli Corsi in Quenza and Muntagne Corse in Liberta, Ajaccio. There are a number of inter-village circuits such as Boziu (east of Corte), Tavaru (southern valleys), Venacais (transhumance trails), Mare and Monte (Calenzana to Cargese), Guagnais and Fra Limonti. Ask Park HQ for details.

Horse-riding. *Centres équestres* are at Venaco (☎ 95.47.01.87), Bastelica (☎ 95.28.71.83) and Calacuccia (☎ 95.48.00.11). Contact also Pineto Lucciana, 20290 Borgo (☎ 95.36.03.27).

Cycling/VTT. Cycles can be rented in Ajaccio, Zonza and Corte.

Canoe/kayak. Ponte-Leccia (24 km north of Corte) (☎ 95.47.62.60).

Caving. (*spéléologie*) There are 200 grottoes and caves to explore. Contact Daniel Santoni, 32 cours Paoli, 20250 Corte (☎ 95.46.02.95).

Skiing. Zicavo has a ski-school and slopes (☎ 95.24.40.44); others are at Quenza (on D420) (☎ 95.78.62.11) and Marignana (☎ 95.26.21.21).

WHAT TO SEE
Museums. Albertacco (archaeology); Cervione (art and folklore); Levie (prehistory); Ajaccio (Bonaparte's house).

Casa Natura da Vizzavona (at Vivario) (☎ 95.47.21.50). A small forest nature museum.

Crafts. See village craft associations' handiwork in Corte, Evisa and Zonza.

Church frescoes. San Nicolao de Sermano; Favalello; San Quilico at Cambia; St-Michel's Oratory at Castirla.

Calasima. At 1004 m, this is the highest village in Corsica; 5 km west of Calacuccia at the foot of Cinto, it has superb views including the amphitheatre of Niolo.

Ajaccio. Cathedral and Bonaparte's house.

Bastia. Citadel, old port and town, ethnological museum.

Calvi. Cathedral, citadel, Moorish village of San-Antonio.

Sartène. Prehistory museum, megalithic stones at Tizzano.

Bonifacio. Citadel, boat trips to Sardinia, nature reserve of Lavezzi.

San-Baizo-Aleria. Roman and Greek antiquities, archaeological museum in Fort Matra.

Basque pelota at San-Nicolao in Poggio (☎ 95.38.52.59).

WHERE TO STAY

No hotels inside the park, but there are *auberges* in some of the villages: Corte, Zonza, Zicavo, Col de Vizzavona, Bastelica and Quenza. For a list of rural *gîtes* consult CAR, 22 bd Dominique Paoli, Ajaccio (☎ 95.22.14.60). Youth hostels are at Alando, Casanova-di-Venaco, Corte, Cozzano, Guitera, Marignana, Osani, Ota, Pianello, Sermano, Venaco and Zivaco. Individual camping is forbidden within the nature park, but there are three campsites at Corte and one at Serra-di-Scopamene.

TOURIST OFFICES

Ajaccio. 1 pl. Foch (☎ 95.21.40.87); 65 cours Napoléon (☎ 95.23.15.01).
Bastia. Pl. St-Nicolas (☎ 95.31.00.89); pl. Vincetti (☎ 95.33.25.80).
Corte. Hôtel de la Paix (near PTT) (☎ 95.46.06.72).
Calvi. Port de Plaisance (☎ 95.65.16.67).

CAMARGUE

Region: PROVENCE

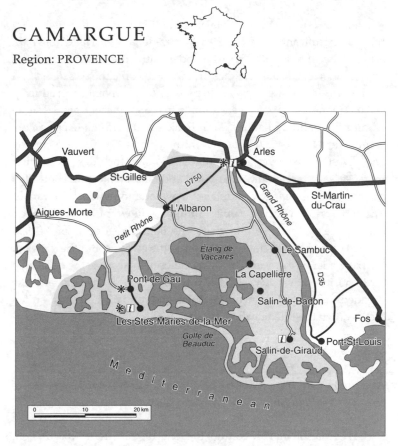

The park was created in 1970 within the Rhône delta and occupies a triangular area of 85,000 ha with Arles at the northern apex and the Mediterranean forming the southern side. The Grand Rhône and Petit Rhône form the eastern and western borders. It is probably the most important wetland area in Europe with 337 varieties of migrant birdlife recorded. The land is very flat and rises only to a maximum height of 9 m. Within the park there are three main nature reserves.

The Réserve Nationale de Vaccarès (13,177 ha), run by the Société Nationale de Protection de la Nature (SNAP), is in the centre, a region of lakes and marshes extending southwards. This is the main state nature reserve.

To the east near Le Sambuc is the private reserve, Tour du Valet (1070 ha), which has a biological station. To the west, the Réserve Départementale des Impériaux et du Malagroy (2777 ha) is on the outskirts of the only significant town, Les Stes-Maries-de-la-Mer. The whole park is a complex mosaic with 28,000 ha under cultivation: mainly rice crops but also maize, wheat and vines, from which come the *vins du sable*. A further 15,000 ha are *salins*, salt pans and salt marshes producing 600,000 tonnes of salt each year, mainly in the southeast from Salin-de-Giraud and Salin-de-Badon. Natural lakes and man-made *plans d'eau* account for a further 13,000 ha, and the remaining 27,000 ha are hunting and livestock reserves. The mixed ecology includes freshwater marshes, salt steppes, brackish pools and lakes, which are controlled by pumping stations to desalinate the water and regulate the canals. Windbreaks of tamarisk, poplar, juniper, willow, pine and bamboo clumps are picturesque and mark the boundaries between 30 *mas* (farms) owned by the traditional Camargue *gardiens*. But the views of the flat wetlands can seem a trifle monotonous except to the dedicated bird and insect watchers. It is windy for much of the year and the dreaded *mistral* – a dry, uncomfortable wind from the northeast – often blows down the Rhône valley.

Maps. Michelin 83; IGN 66, 303.

Access. By road from Arles by N570 via L'Albaron southwest to Les Stes-Maries-de-la-Mer.

Park HQ. Maison du Parc Naturel Régional de Camargue, Mas du Pont de Rousty, rte de Stes-Maries-de-la-Mer, 13200 Arles (☎ 90.97.10.40), and also the Centre d'Information et d'Animation de Ginès (Centre François-Hüe), Pont-de-Gau (☎ 90.97.86.32), 4 km north of Les Stes-Maries-de-la-Mer, 0900–1230, 1400–1800 (except Thur. Oct.–Mar.).

FAUNA

Above all the Camargue is famous for the multitude of wintering migrating and breeding birds on their way to and from North Africa. Nearly 6000 pairs of the greater flamingo, shining pinkly, regularly breed here, as do tern, pratincole, egret and heron, as well as avocet and black-winged stilt. Nearly a quarter of a million ducks winter in the Camargue including mallard, widgeon, pintail, shoveller and gadwall. Waterfowl include garganey and plover. Eight species of gull noted include black-headed and herring. Ten species of tern and common crane can be seen, as well as the unusual European bee-eater, common roller and penduline tit. The Mediterranean beach has breeding Kentish plover and, in the dunes, tawny pipit and short-toed lark. The main flamingo, stilt and avocet breeding areas are in the saline lagoons to the south and near the salt extraction plants to the southeast. The gulls and the terns prefer the saline lagoons to the north. The most visible areas of the great marshes and lagoons which can be seen from roads and paths are full of warblers, herons, egrets, marsh harriers, terns and waders. In the rice-growing areas watch out for whiskered terns, and in the occasional woodland melodious warblers and golden orioles.

Although the migrations take place in spring and autumn there are just as many species to see during the summer (but August should be avoided because of the crowds, heat and mosquitoes).

The 500–600 *gardiens*, who are rugged cowboy-horsemen, manage 5000 small, nippy, black fighting bulls called *manades*, herds of semi-wild white horses (born brown, but turning white after three years), cattle and 80,000 sheep. The transhumance occurs twice a year when the sheep winter in the Camargue and in the spring go up into the Alps.

The wetlands contain lizards, eel, terrapins, watersnakes and tree-frogs. Larger animals that can be spotted are wild boar, beaver, badgers, fox, coypu and rabbits. Freshwater fish include pike and perch, and among the seawater species are sole and bass.

FLORA AND VEGETATION

The coastal sand-dunes and canals have many varieties of shrub, grasses, sea lavender, pondweed, bulrushes, water buttercups and reeds, which are important for waterfowl nesting. It is a grazing area for the cattle, sheep, half-wild horses and fighting bulls. There are artificial islands created to facilitate migrant bird nesting, which is best viewed from the Tour du Valat biological station near Le Sambuc.

Parc Ornithologique. Pont-de-Gau (☎ 90.97.82.62), near the Park HQ. 12 ha of *marais* with dozens of bird species, local and migrant, in their natural habitat, seen from signed paths. Moreover, one of the best walks in the Camargue is through a further 50 ha of marshlands along the west side of the Réserve des Impériaux and Étang du Vaccarès. Open every day 0900–sundown. Fee.

ECOMUSÉES

Musée Camarguais. Mas du Pont de Rousty (☎ 90.97.10.82) near the Maison du Parc. Located in a large old *bergerie* or sheep farm off the N576 10 km southwest of Arles, this museum has all the necessary information – ecological, historical, geological, industrial and traditional – presented and documented in air-conditioned surroundings. This is a plus as the Camargue is very hot and humid in midsummer. There is also a 3½ km walk through typical *marais* marshland. Allow 1½ hours for the visit plus another 1½ hours for the walk (*sentier*). Open 0915–1745 Apr.–Sept., 1015–1645 Oct.–Mar. Closed Tue. Oct.–Mar. Fee.

Réserve Nationale de Camargue. La Capellière (☎ 90.97.00.97), off D36 east of Étang du Vaccarès. This Centre d'Information Nature is near two bird observatories and the start of a 20 km circular walk among the sand-dunes and littoral. An ideal place for ornithologists to visit as flocks of pink flamingos frequent the area. 0900–1200, 1400–1700. Closed Sun. Fee.

Domaine de la Palissade (☎ 42.86.81.28) Off D36 in southeast corner of the Camargue near Port-St-Louis and Salin-de-Giraud. An exhibition building with diorama, aquarium, environmental audiovisuals of flora and fauna of the lagoons of the Basse Camargue, plus three local guided walks of up to 20 km. Midsummer group visits at 0930 and 1430. Sept.–June 0900–1700. Mon.–Fri. Fee.

SALT

The salt marsh areas west towards Aigues-Mortes and east towards Salin-de-Giraud have been worked since the 13thC. From Mar.–Sept. the paddy-fields are flooded one foot deep with salt water and by the end of the hot summer evaporation has left salt crystals which are piled up into huge white, glittering heaps called *camelles* towering to 20 m. These strange man-made hills can be seen in the Crau plain from the N113 between Salon-de-Provence and Arles.

WHAT TO DO

Walks. In this vast, flat, watery wilderness there are many local walks (no Grandes Randonnés) from Les Stes-Maries-de-la-Mer, running north and east of the Étang du Vaccarès. The tourist offices will advise you of the best routes.

Horse-riding. Thirty *mas* (farms) will rent horses by the hour or day (☎ 90.97.84.64 or 90.97.81.09).

Boat trips. From Mar.–Nov. the *Tiki III* sails up the Petit Rhône from the small port 2.5 km west of Les-Stes-Maries-de-la-Mer. The voyage takes 1¼ hours and there are lovely views to be photographed (☎ 90.97.81.68).

Aquatic sports. There are superb bathing, sail- and sand-yachts, and dune exploration along the coastline. The main beaches are Plage de Piémanson (east) and Les Stes-Maries-de-la-Mer (west).

Stages Photo or Safaris Photo. These are rather overpriced but interesting guided photographic tours. Advice from tourist office or ☎ 90.47.89.33.

Mejanes Amusement Centre (☎ 90.97.10.10). Off D570 7 km north of Les Stes-Maries-de-la-Mer.This centre has a wide variety of entertainment, particularly for children: horse rides, mock bullfights, safari tours, etc.

WHAT TO SEE

Château d'Avignon. Off D570 12 km north of Les Stes-Maries-de-la-Mer, this is an imposing 19thC château with Aubusson and Gobelin tapestries, paintings and furnishings of note. The botanical gardens extend for 500 m and contain 28 different varieties of herb. Guided visits 0915, 1030, 1430, 1600 Apr.–Sept. preferably by contacting the Park HQ at Pont de Gau (☎ 90.97.86.32).

Musée Baroncelli. A local history and folklore museum in the old Hôtel de Ville, Les Saintes-Maries-de-la-Mer. 0900–1200, 1400–1800. Closed Wed. Fee.

Musée de Cire du Boumian. Near Ginès on D570. A waxworks museum of the typical Camargue lifestyles. 1000–1900. Closed Tue. Fee.

Fortified church. Les Stes-Maries-de-la-Mer. 9/10thC church with a crypt and relics of the Saints Marie Salomé, Marie Jacobe and Black Sarah, the patroness of the local gypsies. 0900–1200, 1400–1900. Fee.

Bullfights. *Courses à la cocardes* and *courses provençales* are exciting, non-lethal running-of-the-bulls *spectacles* in the various arenas or bullrings. In July and Aug. Tue. and Thur., Sat. p.m. and Sun. p.m. Advice from tourist offices.

WHERE TO STAY

Les Saintes-Maries-de-la-Mer (pop. 2000) is the main town on the coast with many hotels, *pensions*, farmhouses and some *gîtes*. There are also three campsites around Les Stes-Maries: Le Clos du Rhône, La Brise and Le Large. But Arles is much more attractive, has a better choice of hotels and restaurants and superb Roman antiquities, and is half an hour by road from the centre of the Camargue. A youth hostel is in Pioch-Badet on the D570 8 km southwest of Arles (☎ 90.97.91.72).

TOURIST OFFICES

Les Stes-Maries-de-la-Mer. Ave. Van-Gogh (near the *Arènes*) (☎ 90.97.82.55).
Salin-de-Giraud. Mairie annexe (☎ 42.86.80.87).
Arles. 35 pl. de la République (☎ 90.96.29.35).

REGIONAL VISIT

Between the Camargue and Marseille via Fos and Martigues, the *Côte Bleue Regional Park* is at Carry-le-Rouet, which is a pretty little seaside resort and fishing port. It extends 1.6 km off the coast between La Balise-de-l'Ane and Cap de Nantes. The length of coastline is 17.5 km and the area of the park is 3070 ha, of which 70 ha is a marine reserve. Experiments in myticulture with white bream, lobsters, etc., have been carried out, and activities include marine ecology, diving classes and research studies on marine grass, marine benthos, sea urchins and rare fish species. Park HQ: c/o Club de la Mer, Sausset-les-Pins.

CÉVENNES

Region: LANGUEDOC

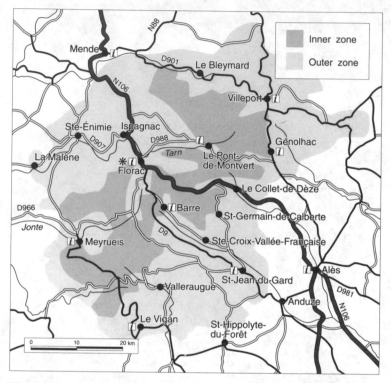

The area of the Cévennes national park is often associated with the travels of Robert Louis Stevenson, who with his donkey Modestine explored the strongholds of the unfortunate Camisard peasants slaughtered in the religious war of 1702. Created in 1970, this is the only one of the six national parks (other than Port-Cros) that is not mountainous, with heights of only 400–1700 m. It is spread over 338,000 ha across the *départements* of Lozère, Gard and Ardèche and occupies the southern sector of the Massif-Central around Florac. The fully protected inner zone has only a few hundred inhabitants, mainly farmers. The outer buffer zone of 237,000 ha has 122 communes with a population of 41,000. The park is heavily wooded with the gorge canyons of the rivers Tarn and Jonte overlooked by Mont Lozère (1700 m), Mont Aigoual (1600 m) and Mont Bouges (1400 m). The river valley corniches are beautiful, with rich and interesting flora and fauna, and the area is still unspoilt, apart from crowded roads in August. It is too easy for travellers to drive through this splendid region without realising what they are missing. Facilities for walks, exploration and lodging are excellent.

Maps. Michelin 80; IGN 58, 59, 65.

Access. St-Flour on N9/N106 to Mende (northwest corner of park). Nîmes northwest on N106 to Alès (southeast corner). From Avignon northwest on D981 to Alès. From Montpellier northwest on N109/N9 to Millau. From St-Étienne/Le Puy south on N88 to Mende. Trains run from Alès to Langogne, La Bastide-Puylaurent and Génolhac. Buses go from Alès to Florac and St-Jean-du-Gard, and from Florac to Mende, Millau and Génolhac.

Park HQ. Information du Parc National is located in the handsome Château de Florac, BP 15, 48400 Florac (☎ 66.49.53.00). 0900–1900. Also there are park information centres at Barre-des-Cévennes, Le Collet-de-Dèze, Génolhac, La Malène, Le Mazel-du-Bleymard, Meyrueis, Mas-Camargues, Le Mont-Aigoual, Le Pont-de-Montvert, St-Germain-de-Calberte, St-Jean-du-Gard, St-Laurent-de-Trèves, Le Vigan, Villefort, Le Pompidou, Ste-Croix-Vallée-Française, Pont-Ravagers, Les Gorges-de-la-Jonte and Col-de-Jalcreste.

The Cévennes is a very large park and is run by an efficient organisation of 60 people, half of whom work in the field. They run the area as mentors and guides, ensuring nature is protected and making scientific observations.

ZONES

Causse Méjean. A limestone plateau, part of the Grand Causses of Sauveterre, Causse Noir and Larzac. The average elevation is 1000 m and sheep grazing is the main activity. It is on the west side of the park between La Malène and Meyrueis with the Gorges du Tarn (D907) to the north and Gorges de la Jonte (D996) to the south.

123

Mont Lozère. A formidable granitic massif which includes the Rocs des Laubies, Pic de Finiels, Rochers du Trenze and Malpertus (Pic Cassini). There is some cattle rearing and sheep transhumance. This is the northern sector of the park between Le Bleymard (D901 from Mende) and Le Pont-de-Montvert (D998 from Florac). There are some fortified farms, menhirs and boundary stones carved with the Camisard Maltese Cross.

Montagne de Bougès. A granite and schistous mountain range wooded on the northern slopes; with forestry, cattle and sheep breeding. The area is east of Florac (N106 through the Gardon valleys).

Valleys of the Gardon rivers. The Vallée Longue watered by the Gardon river from Alès, the Vallée Française by the Gardon from Ste-Croix and the Vallée Borgne by the Gardon from St-Jean. There are sweet-chestnut groves, goat and sheep raising and bee keeping. The area is southwest of Florac and west of Alès and is best visited from the Corniche des Cévennes (D9).

Mont Aigoual and Lingas plateau. A granite and schistous area with forests of pine, spruce, fir and beech. Transhumance of cows and sheep and forestry are the main activities. In the southern region of the park, they are most easily reached from Le Vigan (D190/48) or Valleraugue (D986).

Rivers. Mediterranean watershed: Gardons, Cèze and Hérault. Atlantic watershed: Lot, Tarn, Mimente, Tarnon, Dourbie, Trévezel and Jonte.

FAUNA

There are 45 species of mammal including wild boar, red deer, roe deer, beaver, badger, pine marten, fox, wild cat, Corsican *mouflon* and hare. About 100 deer are in the Vallée Française, 60 around Mont Aigoual, another 60 around Mont Lozère. There are 150 bird species including 100 griffon vultures (*vautours*), 50 lammergeiers (bearded vultures), golden eagles, peregrine falcons, choughs, eagle owls, bustards, alpine swifts, rock thrushes, ortolan buntings, larks, ravens, curlews, harriers and recently black grouse and capercaillie (*grand tétras*). In addition there are 30 reptile and amphibian and 20 freshwater fish species including trout. At Ventzjols is an enclosure for Przewalski horses, a protected species. The Cévennes are particularly proud of their *vautour fauve*, nicknamed *bouldras*, carefully reintroduced in 1967.

FLORA AND VEGETATION

Over 1200 species have been identified including 20 protected plants and alpine flowers (martagon lily, yellow pheasant's eye and 40 species of orchid including lady's slipper). The variety of rock types harbours endemic species and the 1000 peat bogs contain broom, heather, peat moss, sundew and sphagnum. Over 150,000 ha of forest (i.e. 45 per cent of the total area) cover the central and boundary zones of the park. Up to a height of 500 m are holm oaks; from 500–1000 are deciduous oak and sweet chestnut; and from 1000–1500 m are beech and fir. Also to be seen are Scots pine, silver fir and silver birch. In the spring the valleys are covered with white narcissus, wild tulips, pasque flowers, feather grass and wild daffodils.

WHAT TO DO

Walks. The park is ideal for rambles. Serious walkers can choose from the Grande Randonnée 7 (Vosges–Pyrenees), the GR 6 and 60 (Rhone–Cévennes), the GR 66 (78 km tour of the Aigoual), the GR 67 (130 km tour of the Cévennes) and the GR 68 (11 km tour of Mont Lozère). Topoguides are on sale locally. In addition 22 local nature discovery trails have been blazed in the park (leaflets on sale at information centres). In the summer 19 local guided, free, walks are organised by the park authorities (☎ 66.49.53.01), and the wide range vary from 1½ to 6 hours' duration. They are: seven round Mont Lozère, four round Causse Méjean, four round the Cévennes, three round Aigoual, and one introductory walk of 2½ hours which leaves from the Château de Florac. Organised walks start in July and end at the beginning of Sept.

R. L. Stevenson trail. In Sept. 1878 he set out from Le Monastier, south of Le Puy, and walked for 12 days through the deepest Cévennes via Pradelles, Notre-Dame-des-Neiges, Le Bleymard (Montagne du Goulet), Pic-de-Finiels, Pont-de-Montvert, Florac and the Corniche des Cévennes to St-Jean-du-Gard. FIRA, ave. René-Boudon, St-Jean-du-Gard (☎ 66.85.17.94) organise R.L.S. tours.

Grottoes. Visit the grottoes at Le Vigan (Clamouse, Demoiselles), Camprieu/Vallerauge (Dargilan) and Anduze (Trabuc). Permission is needed to pothole and cave at Ispagnac.

Standing stones. Visit menhirs, megaliths and dolmens at Mas-St-Chezy (La Marque), near Florac (Pierre-Plate and Valbelle), at Hures-la-Parade (Goujac) and on the Causse Méjean (Fraisse).

Skiing. Facilities on Mont Lozère and Massif de l'Aigoual (1500 m), ski-school ☎ 67.82.22.78; at Prat-Peyrot (☎ 67.82.60.93); and at Génolhac.

Horse-riding. There are four *centres équestres* around Mont Lozère, one in the Cévennes and three in the Causse-Aigoual sector. Ask tourist offices for the leaflet *Carte d'Invitation à Cheval*. 500 km of bridle-paths are signposted.

Canoe/kayak/rafting. Rental from Ispagnac, Le Pont-de-Montvert, Le Rozier, St-Jean-du-Gard and Florac.

Archery. A centre for this sport is at Florac (Champ Notre-Dame).

Cycling/VTT. Cycles can be hired at the station at Alès, La Bastide-Puylaurent, Langogne, Marvejols, Mende and Villefort.

Steam train. Across the Cévennes from St-Jean-du-Gard to Anduze and back is a 13 km ride with spectacular scenery. The track goes through 4 tunnels, across 10 viaducts and over 20 bridges. TVC Gare St-Jean-du-Gard (☎ 66.85.13.17).

WHAT TO SEE

Museums

Ecomusée du Mont Lozère (☎ 66.45.80.73), at Maison du Mont Lozère, Mas Camargues, Ferme de Troubat and Mas de la Barque.

Musée des Vallés Cévenoles. St-Jean-du-Gard.

Musée Cévenol. 1 rue des Calquières, Le Vigan (☎ 67.81.06.86).

Musée and Maison de la Soie (silk). St-Hippolyte-du-Foret, Apr.–Nov.

Musée 'le Vieux Logis'. Ste-Enimie.

Musée de Cévenol 'l'Homme et Sa Montagne'. Pont-Ravagers.

Musée du Desert. Mialet (☎ 66.85.02.72). Camisard history. July–Aug. 0930-1830.

Musée de la Chataigne (chestnut). Pied-de-Born (Villefort).

Ecomusée de la Vallée du Galcizon Cendras.

Châteaux

*Le Castellas.*Lasalle. Guided visits July–Aug 1330–1830.

*Château de Castanet.*Villefort. 1000–1900.

*Château de Calberte.*St-Germain-de-Calberte. Exhibitions.

Château de Roquedols Meyrueis. Exhibitions.

(Check entry times at tourist offices and expect to pay a small entry fee.)

Exhibitions, etc.

Aumont-Aubrac (north of Mende). Summer exhibitions, craftwork.

Lanuejols. Botanic garden *herbier du Causse Noir*.

Hyelzas (Causse Méjean). Restored *caussenarde* farmhouse.

La Borie (Causse Méjean). Summer exhibitions of prehistory.

Nîmes-le-Vieux (Causse Méjean). Geological exhibitions Apr.–Sept.

Molines. Permanent sculpture, watercolour and art exhibitions.

Anduze. Visit the potteries and the bamboo forest which contains 100 varieties in 35 ha and is unique in Europe.

Ste-Enimie. Visit the medieval village. Tue., Thur. p.m.

Dinosaur footprints of 190 million years back are at St-Laurent-de-Trèves 10 km south of Florac (N107).

Natural sights. A 38 km tour can be made of the ridges by D998 from Génolhac to Les Bastides, back via D35 and D906. One of the best viewpoints is Col de l'Hospitalet, south of St-Laurent-de-Trèves. But best of all is to travel by canoe through the Gorges du Tarn or to walk through the gorge on the D907bis from Le Rozier to Ste-Enimie.

TWINNING

The Cévennes park is twinned with Montseny reserve in Catalonia, Spain, and with Saguenay national park in Quebec, Canada.

WHERE TO STAY

Florac in the centre of the park has several small hotels and has the Park HQ in the town château. Other possibilities at Ste-Enimie, Meyrueis, St-Jean-du-Gard, Génolhac, Villefort, Le Vigan and Bagnols-les-Bains.

There are *auberges* at Cabrillac, L'Hospitalet and La Croix-de-Berthel. Ask at tourist offices for a list of *gîtes, chambres d'hôte, camping à la ferme* and campsites. For instance Florac, Ispagnac and Meyrueis have 4 sites each. A youth hostel is at St-Etienne-Vallée-Française (Le Merlet, Le Pont du Burgon).

TOURIST OFFICES

Florac. Ave. J.-Monestier (a.m. only) (☎ 66.45.01.14).

Mende. 16 bd Soubeyran (☎ 66.65.02.69); 3 rue Chapitre (☎ 66.49.20.54).

Millau. Ave. A.-Merle (☎ 65.60.02.42).

Alès. 2 rue Michelet (☎ 66.78.49.10); pl. G.-Péri (☎ 66.52.32.15).

Le Vigan. Pl. Marché (☎ 67.81.01.72).

There are small offices at St-Jean-du-Gard (☎ 66.85.10.48); Génolhac (☎ 66.61.10.55); Villefort (☎ 66.46.80.26); Meyrueis (☎ 66.45.62.81); Barre-des-Cévennes (☎ 66.45.05.07); Le Pont-de-Montvert (☎ 66.45.84.77).

HAUT-LANGUEDOC

Region: LANGUEDOC

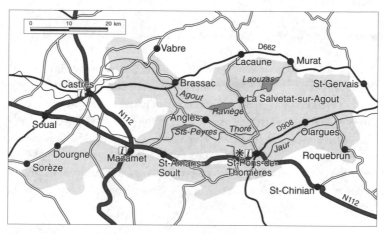

Created in 1973, the Parc Naturel Régional du Haut-Languedoc is at the southwest extremity of the Massif-Central. It extends over the *départements* of Tarn and Hérault, east of Toulouse, north of Carcassonne and Narbonne, west of Montpellier and south of Albi. Consisting of 145,000 ha, it has 70 communes and 70,000 inhabitants and there are six distinct areas: Les Monts de Lacaune in the north, L'Espinouse in the northeast, Sidobre in the northwest, Menervois and Montagne Noire in the south, Le Somail in the southeast and Le Caroux in the east, all part of a mountain massif (maximum height 1100 m) with lush green uplands, rocky crags and gorges, over a third of which is heavily wooded. The park is watered by the rivers Agout, Thoré, Mare, Orb and Jaur, and the large lakes of Laouzas, Raviège, Sts-Peyres and Laprade-Basse are fed by fast-flowing mountain streams. The main towns in the park are Mazamet, southeast of Castres on the N112, and St-Pons-de-Thomières, 35 km east of Mazamet. Small rural industries include clothmaking, granite extraction, woodworking, forestry, iron and copperwork, winemaking at St-Pons, glassmaking and many other groups of craft activity. The casual traveller may drive from Castres on the N112 via Mazamet and later St-Pons-de-Thomières towards Béziers or Montpellier without realising that the delights of the park are to the

129

north via minor roads D93, D622, D68 and D907 and to the south by D118, D920 and D907. It is a region full of history: it was on the pilgrim route to Santiago de Compostela and became a refuge in the religious persecutions of Cathars and Huguenots and more recently for the World War II resistance.

Maps. Michelin 82, 83, 86; IGN 63, 64, 2244, 2343, 2344, 2443, 2444.

Access. Road access from the west (Castres, Albi) and from the east (Béziers) is easy by the N112 and D908 from Montpellier. From the north it is difficult, which adds great charm to the main area of the park, rarely visited by tourists. Approach from the south via Carcassonne is also difficult, except by D118. The railway from Toulouse-Matabiau reaches Castres and Mazamet and meanders eastwards past St-Pons and Olargues on its way southeast to Béziers and northeast to Millau. Buses travel between Toulouse and St-Pons; from Montpellier to La Salvetat and Bédarieux.

Park HQ. Maison du Parc, 13 rue du Clôtre, St-Pons-de-Thomières, 34220 Hérault (☎ 67.97.02.10) is the HQ with a whole range of activities and information available. There are also Maisons du Parc at Brassac, 81260 Tarn (☎ 63.74.01.29); Fraisse-sur-Agout, Prat-Alaric (☎ 67.97.64.46); Roquebrun, Les Moulins (☎ 67.89.64.54); Nages, Rieu-Montagné (☎ 63.37.45.76); and Sorèze (☎ 63.74.16.28). Most of these Maisons du Parc, including Brassac, Rieu-Montagné and Sorèze, have archaeological sites, exhibitions and a *centre culturel*.

FAUNA

Besides a thousand wild sheep (*mouflon*), herds of goats and domestic sheep, there are red fox, weasel and small mammals to be seen, and in the hills there are rare breeding raptors – royal eagles, St Martin buzzards, grey buzzards and Grand-Duc owls, and plenty of hawks (*genette*). They feed on the many varieties of reptile – snakes and lizards – seen in *l'arrière pays*. In the rivers and streams are eel, crayfish, bleak, barbel, as well as trout, perch and bream. A hunting reserve between Rosis and Cambon near the Caroux massif is closed to the public.

FLORA AND VEGETATION

In the regions with ocean winds and rain (Sidobre and Montagne Noire) expect to see broom and heathlands, forests of beech (including Pic de Nore) and firs as well as Pyrenean-style plants such as yellow lilies and scylla. In the southwest of the park where the vegetation is more Mediterranean, there are oaks and sweet chestnuts. In the humid gorges there are birch, alder, willow, ash and poplars. But in the lush fields alongside the N112 there are the usual oats, barley, wheat and grazing land.

ECOLOGY

CPIE at Salvetat-sur-Agout (☎ 67.97.02.10) and the Maisons du Parc at St-Pons and Brassac offer practical ecology studies on the Montagne Noire, Caroux massif and Somail region. The biology laboratory at Douch on the Caroux massif offers ecology courses (*stages*) (☎ 67.97.02.10).

WHAT TO DO

Walks. There are many possibilities with six Grandes Randonnées crossing the park. The GR 7 from the Vosges to the Pyrenees takes in Lamalou-les-Bains and Arfons. The GR 653 goes from St-Gervais-sur-Mare to Revel; the GR 76 from Plô-du-Four to Verdun-Lauragais; the GR 77 from Saut-de-Vésoles to Minerve; the GR 36 from Albi to Pic de Nore and the GR 71 from Murat-sur-Vèbre to Rialet. The historical route of the pilgrims to Compostela followed the GR 653 from St-Gervais in the northeast westwards through Murat and La Salvetat on the way to Castres. There are probably as many good walks in this park as in any other in France.

Minibus tours. During midsummer these are available from every Maison du Parc.

Caving (*spéléologie*). Consult the Maison du Parc, Mairie de Roquebrun, Cessenon (☎ 67.89.64.54).

Horse-riding. There are *centres équestres* at Brassac, Les Cammazes,

Labastide-Rouairoux, Montredon-Labessonié, St-Gervais-sur-Mare, La Salvetat-sur-Agout and Vabre.

Cycling/VTT. 600 km of trails around the small villages is suggested by the Maisons du Parc.

Donkey trails. A trained ass (*âne bâté*) can be hired from Prémian near Olargues (Le Poujol) (☎ 67.97.06.05). Great fun for children.

Sporting activities. There are four *bases de loisirs* at Mons-la-Trivalle, Lac de Laouzas, La Salvetat-sur-Agout and Moulin de Tarassac.

Skiing. Not highly developed, but there are 7 small resorts with 200 km of marked *pistes*. Ask for the leaflet *Ski de Fond* at the Maisons du Parc.

Canoe/kayak. The rivers Orb and Jaur provide good opportunities.

Swimming. In the lakes in midsummer. Ask Maisons du Parc for details.

Spas. Take the waters at Lamalou-les-Bains and Lacaune.

WHAT TO SEE

Natural sights. The famous Gorges d'Héric in the Sidobre valley off the D98 near Olargues.

The valley of the river Agout with the lakes of Laouzas and Raviège.

The Caroux massif called the *montagne de lumière* off the D908 north of Lamalou-les-Bains.

The Sidobre valley near Castres with its granite plateau north of the D622.

The 1210 m Pic de Nore, the highest of the Montagne Noire range is southeast of Mazamet.

Waterfalls and cascades along the rivers Caroux and Lignon and at the Lac de Vézoles.

The grottoes at Devèze 5 km from St-Pons.

Architecture. 12–18thC fortified church in St-Pons; royal military school at Sorèze; 15thC Hôtel de Ville and château at St-Amans-Soult; 11–16thC Château de Ferrières; 16thC arcades and 15–17thC church at Dourgne; and 13thC Maison d'Adelaide at Burlats.

Museums

Ferrières. Museum of Protestant movement in Haut-Languedoc, next to Château de Ferrières, June–Sept.

Mazamet. La Mémoire de la Terre museum in Maison Fuzier.

Sorèze. Archaeological museum in Maison du Parc.

Rieu-Montagné. Geology and archaeology museum in Maison du Parc, June–Sept.

St-Gervais-sur-Mare. Folklore museum in Maison Cévenole.

St-Pons. Museum of Roman art in Chapelle des Pénitents.

Les Moulins de Roquebrun. Painting and folklore exhibitions.

L'Espinouse. Traditional farm at Prat-Alaric (mill, forge), Aug. only.

Some museums open only in midsummer months, usually open 1000-1200. Most charge a fee.

Festivals. The region has a good musical reputation and groups such as *Musiciens de la Talvern* play traditional songs and music. Lamalou-les-Bains has a three-month operetta season and summer concerts are given at Mamazet, Minerve, Sorèze and Ferrière. Local *fêtes* are held in every village at the end of summer, but try Lacaune (*charcuterie*), St-Chinian (wine), Anglès (woodworking), Olargues, Murat-sur-Vèbre, Sorèze and Lamalou-les-Bains. Ask at the tourist office for a list of *fêtes et spectacles*.

Crafts. There are 42 associations within the park. Durfort, for instance, has *olinandiers* (leatherworkers) and a traditional metalbeating iron hammer. There are exhibitions of local skills at Dourgne, La Salvetat, Roquebrun, St-Gervais-sur-Mare and Vabre.

Megaliths and dolmens. Consult the Maison du Parc at Rieu-Montagné, Mairie de Nages (☎ 63.37.40.48). Also visit the Lac de Laouzas in the northeast which has an exhibition and details of all archaeological finds plus a *centre d'accueil*. Along the Tarn valley are a dozen or more dolmens.

WHERE TO STAY

The Maisons du Parc have a list of the many campsites available. The best are near the Lacs de la Ravlège and Laouzas. There are 16 *gîtes d'étape*, many *chambres d'hôte, camping à la ferme* and modest hotels in St-Pons-de-Thomières, Mazamet and Castres.

TOURIST OFFICES

St-Pons-de-Thomières. SI (☎ 67.97.06.65).
Mazamet. Maison Fusier (☎ 63.61.27.07).
Castres. Théâtre Municipal (☎ 63.59.92.44).

REGIONAL VISITS

Albi, the prefecture town of the Tarn with its cathedral and museums, is to the northwest. It was the centre of the Albigensian religious movement (11–13thC).

Castres. West of the park with interesting museums.

Béziers with its ancient cathedral and bullfights is 50 km to the southeast.

St-Chinian is the start of the main Languedoc wine-growing area 23 km southeast.

Carcassonne. This superb walled old city is 20 km due south.

CAR TOURS

Three are recommended:

La Route de l'Espinouse between St-Pons and St-Gervais-sur-Mare.

The two valley routes of La Salvetat–Béziers and La Salvetat–Castres.

PYRÉNÉES-OCCIDENTALES

Region: THE PYRENEES

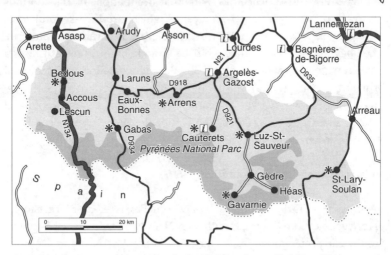

The Pyrenees are a mountain chain 400 km long dividing France and Spain between the Atlantic and the Mediterranean. Along a 100 km stretch southeast of the Basque country, well west of Andorra, lies the Parc National des Pyrénées-Occidentales. It is one of the six national parks created in 1967 mainly because it is of outstanding beauty, has a negligible population to support it and offers enormous recreational potential for rock climbing, skiing, walking, canoe/kayak and horse-riding. Its flora and fauna rank with the best of the French parks and it is physically twinned with the Spanish national park of Ordesa and Mont Perdu. The French park occupies 45,700 ha including the nature reserve of Néouvielle (2300 ha), while the Spanish park has an area of 15,000 ha plus 100,000 ha of hunting reserves. The park is long and narrow, covering altitudes from 1100 m up to 3298 m. Six distinct valleys are a major feature. From west to east they are those of the rivers Aspe, Ossau, Azun, Cauterets, Luzgavarnie and Aure, and two main sights are the glacial amphitheatres called the Cirque de Gavarnie, which has a 423 m waterfall, and the Cirque de Troumouse to the northeast of Gavarnie. The outer perimeter of the park extends to 206,000 ha containing 86 communes of 40,000 inhabitants and includes the small towns of Argelès-Gazost, Cauterets, Gavarnie and Lescun.

135

The nearest large towns are Oloron-Ste-Marie to the northwest and Lourdes to the northeast. After the treaty of Bretigny in 1360 the English owned this area of the Pyrenees for about 90 years, and several villages have historical links with that occupation. In the foothills farmers depend on sheep and cattle which produce several local cheeses. The Pyrenean wine producers are at Jurançon, Madiran, Lembeyre, Béarn and Bellocq, but La Grande Bigourdane at Luz is a 'park' wine. As there are over 230 lakes above 340 m and scores of rushing streams (*gaves*), freshwater trout can be caught for the table. Rainfall is above average, so come equipped with waterproofs and strong shoes also bring camera and binoculars in case you can spot an elusive brown bear.

Maps. Michelin 42, 85; IGN 70, 273–6.

Access. From Tarbes southeast by D935 via Bagnères-de-Bigorre to the Aure valley. From Lourdes south by N21 and D921 via Luz-St-Sauveur to the Gavarnie valley. From Lourdes southeast by N21 and D918 via Argelès-Gazost to the Arens valley. From Pau south on N134/D934 to Laruns and the Ossau valley. From Oloron-Ste-Marie south on N134 to Lescun and the Aspe valley. SNCF stations are at Oloron-Ste-Marie, Lourdes, Argelès-Gazost, Tarbes, Bagnères-de-Bigorre, Ossau, Laruns and Luz. There are several local, rather slow and intermittent bus services out of the main towns. Airports are at Tarbes, Ossun and Pau-Uzein.

Park HQ. The main HQ is at 59 rte de Pau, BP 1316, 65013 Tarbes (☎ 62.93.30.60). Since Tarbes is well north of the park there is sensibly a Maison du Parc in each of the valleys, all with an excellent range of literature in several languages. From west to east they are:

Vallée d'Aspe. 64490 Bedous on N134 south of Oloron-Ste-Marie (☎ 59.34.88.30).

Vallée d'Ossau. Gabas, 64440 Laruns on D934 south of Pau (☎ 59.05.32.13).

Vallée d'Azun. Arrens-Marsous, 65400 Argelès-Gazost on N21/D918 southwest of Lourdes (☎ 62.97.02.66).

Vallée de Cauterets. 65110 Cauterets, on D920 south of Lourdes (☎ 62.92.52.56).

Vallée de Luz. 65120 Gavarnie on D921 under the Cirque de Gavarnie (☎ 62.92.49.10).

Also Vallée de Luz. 65120 Luz-St-Sauveur on D921 26 km north of Gavarnie (☎ 62.92.87.05).

Vallée d'Aure. 65170 St-Lary-Soulan on D929 south of Lannemezan (☎ 62.39.40.91).

Another useful address is CIMES (Centre Information Montagne et Sentiers), 3 square Galagué, 09200 St-Girons (☎ 61.66.40.10), which provides courses, tours and information about ecological activities in the mountains.

The main roads within the park are on a north–south axis. The minor lateral roads, e.g. the D918 and D147, present a challenge.

FAUNA

About 25 *ours bruns* (brown Pyrenean bears), the last colony in France, live in the valleys of the Aspe and Ossau, but are highly protected and rarely seen. There are lynx, ibex, wild boar, deer, the cat-like genets, martens, fox, stoat, badger, wild cat and, near streams, the rare Pyrenean desman, a mole with rat-like tail, horned with webbed feet. The Pyrenean chamois is thriving, with over 9000 at the last count, near Cauterets, La Fruitière and Lac d'Estom. Up to 2000 m the reptile species include grass-snakes and lizards and, above 2000 m, salamanders, toads and vipers. There are said to be 1000 varieties of beetle, 200 species of spider, 50 kinds of centipede and 300 types of butterfly including the apollo. Predictably the bird population is interesting and varied, with capercaillie, 8 pairs of golden eagle, 45 pairs of griffon vulture, 8 pairs of Egyptian vulture and 8 pairs of large bearded vulture. Also one can spot buzzards, falcons, partridges, woodpeckers and owls, as every French bird species has taken refuge in the Pyrenees. The *réserve naturelle de Néouvielle* is situated at the east end of the park between the valleys of the Aure and Luz, east of Luz-St-Sauveur. The lakes and streams contain salmon, trout, perch, eel, brochet, gudgeon and bream.

FLORA AND VEGETATION

About 12 per cent of the park is forested, mainly with beech, oak, fir and pitch pine plus some birch, rowan and willow. Mountain pine forests grow up to an altitude of 2600 m, the highest in Europe. Alpine rose forms a dwarf-shrub layer and rhododendrons grow wild on the sub-alpine moorland. There are 400 indigenous species to be found including ramonda, fritillary, long-leaved saxifrage with white spikes, Pyrenean sea-holly, Pyrenean pheasant's eye, yellow turk-cap lily, Pyrenean gentian and edelweiss. The flowering season is in June–July when the snows have melted and at high altitude in August. Visit the botanical garden of Gavarnie, rte du Cirque, which has 400 species of labelled local flora.

NATURAL SIGHTS

Opinions vary, but the shortlist of the most beautiful natural sights includes the two lakes of Néouvielle and Ayous, the high cirques of Gavarnie and Troumouse, the lakes and waterfalls of Cauterets, including the Pont d'Espagne cascade, the high valley of the Aspe, the Pic du Midi d'Ossau, the Col de Vignemale and the Pic de Balaïtous.

WHAT TO DO

Walks. There are 350 km of signed walks, including the Haute Randonnée Pyrénéenne, which is strictly for very experienced walkers. The Grande Randonnée 10 runs along the higher slopes of 2000–2500 m marked by red/white bands with seven *gîtes d'étape* and *refuges* at Arlet, Ayous, Migouelou, Ichéou, Espuguettes and Barroude, again for trained walkers, but less nerve-racking than the Haute Randonnée! High mountain walk guides and *courses* are available from Compagnie des Guides Pyrénéens at: Ossau (☎ 59.05.37.81); Luz (☎ 62.92.87.28); Garrens (☎ 62.97.00.25) and Aure (☎ 62.39.41.11). CIMES Pyrénées of St-Girons (☎ 61.66.40.10) offers 81 guided walks in the Pyrenees from mid-April–mid-Nov., of which a third are in the national park. Fee.

The Maisons du Parc at St-Lary, Luz, Cauterets, Arrens, Gabas and Etsaut organise free walks, but you must sign up the evening before. For instance you can discover the fauna and flora in the Géla valley or the nature reserve of Néouvielle. Ask for the leaflet *Promenades et Randonnées dans les Hautes Pyrénées* available from most tourist offices.

Horse-riding. *Centres équestres* at Bious-Artigues, Accous, St-Pé and St-Lary. Relais d'Herel of Bagnères-de-Bigorre, La Balaguère of Argelès-Gazost and Chevauchée Pyrénées of Gavarnie offer extensive 4–8 day inclusive *sentiers à cheval*.

Alpinisme. Several guides offer their services for *escalade* and *alpinisme*. Cauterets (☎ 62.92.50.27); Luz-St-Sauveur (☎ 62.92.87.28); Argelès-Gazost (☎ 62.97.00.25); St-Lary-Soulan (☎ 62.39.41.11).

Cycling/VTT. There is a cycle crossing of 6 cols above 2000 m. Cycle clubs are at Gèdre, Argelès and Arudy. Information from Club Cyclo-tourisme, Vic-en-Bigorre (☎ 62.96.72.25).

Caving (*spéléologie*). Some of the most challenging caves are to be found along the chain of Pyrenean mountains. Consult CIMES Pyrénées (☎ 61.66.40.10) for details of Maison des Gouffres and Pic Peric. Also the Comité Départemental de Spéléologie, Lannemezan (☎ 62.98.13.07) will give advice.

Canoe/kayak. Several rivers are practicable – from Etsaut to Bedous in the Gave d'Aspe (14 km), Bedous to Asasp (16 km), Asasp to Oloron (9 km) and on the Gave d'Ossau from Laruns to Louvie-Juzon (17 km). Information from the Comité Départementale de Canoë-Kayak, rue des Arribans, 65200 Gèdre, or bases at Labatut (☎ 62.96.46.28) and Genos-Loudenvieille (☎ 62.99.68.02).

Fishing. Trout fishing in the *gaves* and lakes is popular, but a permit is needed. Ask the Maison du Parc.

Hang-gliding. Courses at Lavedan and elsewhere. Ask Maison du Parc for details.

Skiing. There are ten ski centres at Arrens-Marsous, Barèges, Cauterets, Gavarnie, Hautacam, La Mongie, Luz-Ardiden, Piau-Engaly, St-Lary and Val-Louron. Of these, Barèges is the largest, La Mongie is the smartest, Cauterets is the top ranking with a cable car and St-Lary is the most modern. Information from CPIE, 65200 Bagnères-de-Bigorre (☎ 62.95.03.47) or from Maisons du Parc locally.

Tourist train. The highest in Europe runs for 10 km at over 2000 m from Artouste via Col de l'Ours, Seous and Ormielas up to Lac d'Artouste. For bookings ☎ 59.05.36.99 or 59.05.31.41.

Spas. There are seven *stations thermales* for a variety of *cures*, at Argelès-Gazost, Bagnères-de-Bigorre, Barèges, Beaucens, Capvern-les-Bains, Cauterets and Luz-St-Sauveur. Cauterets dates from the 16thC and is the largest of the spa centres, but Luz-St-Sauveur is more attractive. Information from the tourist offices.

Mule ride. The route follows a special track from the village of Gavarnie 5 km up to the amphitheatre of the enormous Cirque de Gavarnie.

WHAT TO SEE

Villages. The prettiest are Arreau (Quartier St-Exupère), St-Savin with its fortified Romanesque church, Luz-St-Sauveur with the 13thC Knights Hospitalier church, St-Lary-Soulan old town and Argelès-Gazost old town.

Crafts. There are many: working in wood at Arcizans-Dessus, Gelos and Louvie-Guzon, metal at Ste-Colombe, ivory at Gavarnie-Ville, leather at Pragnères, making berets at Oloron-Ste-Marie, spinning in Buziet-Ogeu and Esquièze-Serre, making cattle-bells at Nay and cheese making at Arrens and Laruns.

Fêtes. Every village has a *fête*, usually with a *course à la montagne* open to all comers, perhaps also *pelote basque* and *danses et bals folkloriques*. Laruns and Luz have a series of *fêtes* during Aug./Sept.

Grottoes. You can explore half a dozen, including Bétharram, Médous, Gargas, Labastide (Aspugue) and Lannemezan (Puyo-Pelat). Information from Maisons du Parc.

Bears. The Maison du Parc at Etsaut (☎ 59.34.88.30) organises bear-spotting tours: the animals are rarely seen. One is in captivity in the village of Borce.

Birds of prey. At the Château de Beaucens near Argelès there are demonstrations of birds of prey flying in their natural habitat. Details from the Maison du Parc.

Museums. Bagnères-de-Bigorre has the Musées Bigourdan (folklore) and Salies (*beaux-arts*), and also there is the Arrens-Marsous museum at Plan-d'Aste (botany and geology).

Abbey. The Cistercian abbey of Escaladieu, the second oldest in France, is near the hamlet of Bonnemazon on the D938 northeast of Bagnères-de-Bigorre.

WHERE TO STAY

There are campsites at Arcizanz-Avant, Arreau, Esquièze, St-Pé, Vieille-Aure and Laruns. There is a youth hostel in Tarbes and another at Luz-St-Sauveur. Within the park there are 30 *refuges* each with 30–40 beds July–Sept. and good-value *repas*, but reservations are essential. Down in the valley villages there are *gîtes d'étape* with 15 places, each open all the year, many of them on the GR 10 route. Addresses can be obtained from CIMES (☎ 61.66.40.10). There are hotels in all the spa towns in every price range.

TOURIST OFFICES

Argelès-Gazost (☎ 62.97.00.25). Bagnères-de-Bigorre (☎ 62.95.01.62). Cauterets (☎ 62.92.50.27). Gavarnie (☎ 62.92.49.10). Lannemezan (☎ 62.98.08.31). Lourdes (☎ 62.94.15.64).

REGIONAL VISITS

Lourdes. The famous pilgrimage site has grottoes, a 14thC *château-fort*, the Gavarnie tower, many churches and four museums with souvenirs of Bernadette Soubirous.

Tarbes. The cathedral of Notre-Dame-de-la-Sède dates from the 12thC, and there are the 14thC cloisters in Jardin Massey, the national stud (*haras*) and three interesting museums.

Spanish park. Visit the Ordesa national park by road, the D118/D173 from Arreau and St-Lary-Soulan through the Bielsa tunnel.

LANDES DE GASCOGNE

Region: GASCONY

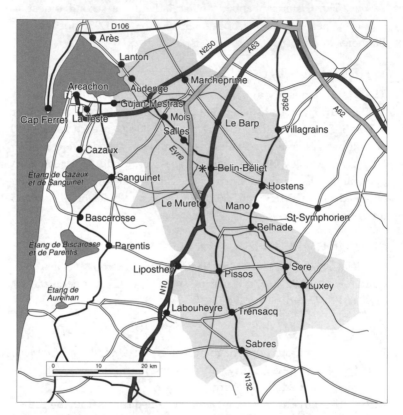

Situated on the west coast of France, this park has its northern edge 20 km southwest of Bordeaux and it extends for 60 km in a southeasterly direction from the Arcachon basin to Sabres. The region of Landes de Gascogne was owned by England for three centuries until 1453. The Parc Naturel Régional des Landes was created in 1970 and comprises 206,000 ha with 22 communes and 30,000 inhabitants, spread evenly over the two *départements* of Gironde and Landes. Included are the nature reserves of Teich (120 ha) and Banc d'Arguin (300 ha). It is off the beaten track, since most tourists drive from Bordeaux to the Spanish frontier by the A63/N10 without realising that the nature park is on both sides of them – unexplored. Essentially a flat sandy terrain with dunes and salt marshes, it has 160,000 ha of forest (80 per cent of the land area), no hills, some excellent beaches and many ecological activities which need tracking down. There are two main rivers – the Eyre and Petite Leyre, the former of which feeds into the delta of Teich in the huge Bassin d'Arcachon southwest of Bordeaux – and half a dozen minor rivers/streams which flow into the Étangs de Cazaux et de Sanguinet, Biscarosse et de Parentis, and Aureilhan. The vast array of pinewoods is rather monotonous, and visitors should be wary of annual fires which destroy about 35,000 ha despite firebreaks and other precautions. It was Napoleon III who in 1857 created a law to make the Landes the biggest forest in Europe. This means that the economy is based on forestry, the production of conifer resins for petrochemicals and, to a lesser extent, pottery, iron and forgeworks – and tourism. There is little grazing land, but one of the side-effects is that a superb protected area is created for migrant birds. There are a dozen villages in the area but no towns, although the Biscay resorts and beaches are half an hour's drive to the west. Nevertheless there are many places to explore as well as extensive educational possibilities for children.

Maps. Michelin 78, IGN 55.

Access. The easiest routes radiate out from Bordeaux: west on D106 to Arès and the isthmus of Cap Ferret; the N250 southwest to Archachon (pop. 14,000). The A63 heads south towards Bayonne, with the N10 as an alternative route. The N134 from Mont-de-Marsan and the D947 from Dax lead northwards to the park. The Paris–Hendaye train stops at Labouheyre and Morcenx (change for Mont-de-Marsan). A small picturesque train chugs from Labouheyre to Marquèze on the *ecomusée* route. Many bus services run between Bordeaux, Dax and Mont-de-Marsan.

Park HQ. Bureau du Parc, pl. de l'Église, 33830 Belin-Béliet (☎ 56.88.06.06) is on the N10 crossroads with D3 (Exit 21 from A63), 38 km south of Bordeaux. There is also an office at 15 pl. Jean-Jaurès, 4000 Mont de Marsan (☎ 58.06.24.25).

FAUNA

There are no notable mammals apart from deer, boar, foxes and some unproductive sheep. But there are 260 bird species including gulls, geese, waders, herons, egrets and duck. Nesting birds include sandwich terns, of which 2000 pairs have been seen at Banc d'Arguin, teal and oyster-catchers. Overwintering species include four species of gull, grey plover and bar-tailed godwit. The delta of the Teich in the southeast corner of the Bassin d'Arcachon is an ornithological park of 120 ha, created in 1972. The most recent success is 100 white spoonbills returning to Le Teich for the first time in four centuries after spending the summer in Holland and the winter in North Africa. Situated in the village of Gujan-Mestras, the Parc Ornithologique, 33470 Le Teich (☎ 56.22.84.89) is open daily 1000–1800 Mar.–Sept., weekends rest of the year. Fee to enter, cabins for photography, guided visits.

Many freshwater fish are to be found in the rivers in the park including eel, trout, perch and pike. There are bees which produce good honey.

FLORA AND VEGETATION

The pine, which was planted in the 19thC, is the most common tree, and some sweet chestnuts and oaks are to be found. Along the river banks are poplar, alder and willow. The marshes (*marais*), lagoons and river deltas have rich aquatic flora, and on the dunes are varieties of marram grass, sand couch and sea holly. The old mine workings are being replanted and recolonised by the park specialists. At Marquèze there is a reserve of tree species and all fruit trees and crops grown in the park. Asparagus and strawberry crops are also grown.

ECOMUSÉES

La Grande Lande. 40630 Sabres (☎ 58.07.52.70). Open all week June–Sept., weekends rest of year. Access is only by the little train leaving from Sabres station nine times a day (roughly once an hour) *en route* for Commensacq and Labouheyre. Sabres is on a crossroads of the N134/D626/D44 46 km south of the Park HQ in Belin-Béliet. The *ecomusée* is a 19thC village with wattle and wooden houses and barns, mill, river, gardens, sheep, bees, henhouse – that is an exact replica of peasant life of the period. Fee.

Atelier de Produits Résineux. 40430 Luxey (☎ 58.08.01.39). Run by the Vidal family, this *ecomusée* in three buildings was an active resin distillery from 1859 to 1954. Now restored, it shows the visitor the machines and multiplicity of end products (oils, perfumes, papers, panels, etc.). Open all week June–Sept., weekends rest of year, guided visits seven times a day, on the hour. Fee.

Maison des Artisans. Maison Marginié, Route de Sore, 40410 Pissos (☎ 58.07.70.66). Pissos is at the crossroads of N134/D43 halfway between the Park HQ and Sabres. 1000–2000 May–Sept. Free. Permanent exhibition by local craftsmen of sabots, honey, wickerwork, waxworks/candle making, pottery, leatherwork, paintings, food products, etc.

Atelier-gîte. Saugnac, 40410 Pissos (☎ 58.07.73.01) offers sophisticated ecology courses for students.

WHAT TO DO

Walks. Unusually there are no Grandes Randonnées but plenty of short local walks. Ask at the Park HQ or tourist offices. The Grande Lande Marathon takes place on 14 July.

Horse-riding. There are *centres équestres* at: Volcelest-Joué, 3380 Belin-Béliet; Tambour Le Caplanne, 33770 Salles; Equilittoral-Bilos, 3370 Salles; Cercle Hippique des Pins, 33830 Le Barp; Petite Leyre, 40410 Belhade; and Ranch d'Elvire, Domaine de Peyricat, Carot, 40630 Sabres.

Swimming. Large pools are open in summer at Sabres, Pissos and Sore.

Canoe/kayak. 100 km of rivers starting from Bassin d'Arcachon and ending at Sabres make an excellent family canoeing holiday. Rentals at Le Teich, Mios, Salles, Le Graox, Testarouman, Pouloye and Mexico. There are ten stops for meals, camping or *gîtes*, and the opportunity to see the river flora and fauna.

Cycling/VTT. There is a 33 km circuit of the park. Consult *atelier-gîte* at Saugnac, 40410 Pissos (☎ 58.07.73.01). Rentals from Mexico (☎ 58.07.05.15).

Fishing. The Domaine Départemental, 33125 Hostens (☎ 56.88.53.22) has a *village des vacances* and 300 ha of lakes, ponds and streams where fishing is authorised. At ten villages *cartes de pêche* (fishing permits) can be purchased. Consult the Mairie at Pissos.

WHAT TO SEE

Traditional Gascon music. Centre Lapios, St-Vital, 33800 Belin-Beliet (☎ 56.88.10.08).

Churches. Argelouse (15thC); Audenge priory; Belhade (11–14thC); Belin-Béliet (pilgrim church, fountain and cemetery); Commensacq (15thC frescoes); Lugos (Vieux Lugo 11thC); Mios (16thC windows); Moustey (two Gothic churches); Pissos (12thC); Sabres; Sore; Trensacq. The pilgrim route to Santiago de Compostela went straight through the park.

Châteaux. Rather modest Rochefort-Lavie at Belhade, and Ruat at Le Teich.

Courses Landaises. Gascon fighting cows perform in arenas through the summer, exciting but non-lethal. Details from Fédération des Courses Landaises, 7 rue des Archers, 40104 Dax.

Museums. Moustey (summer only). Solférino, Musée Napoléon III (☎ 58.07.21.08).

Fairs/fêtes. Held in every village from Easter onwards. Details from Park HQ or tourist offices. Look out for Gascon dances, songs and shepherd stilt-walking events held on Bastille Day, 14 July.

Nature reserves. Banc d'Arguin, La Teste (Gironde); Étang de Cousseau-Lacanau (Gironde); Courant d'Huchet, Léon (Landes); Étang Noir, Seignosse (Landes); Marais des Bruges (near Bordeaux); Près Salés d'Arès-Lège, Arès (Gironde).

Roulotte. Explore by horse-drawn caravan. Atelier Haute-Lande, 40430 Sore (☎ 58.08.01.33).

WHERE TO STAY

There are two holiday villages at Sabres and Hostens and the park offers accommodation in the hamlets of Mexico, Pissos, Testarouman, Saugnac and Le Graoux, which includes campsites, *gîtes ruraux*, etc. There are *auberges* in the northern Gironde sector in Audenge, Belin-Béliet, Biganos, Hostens, Mios, Salles and Le Teich and in the southern Landes sector at Luxey, Pissos, Sabres, Saugnac, Sore and Solférino. There are 13 campsites (8 in Gironde, 5 in Landes) and *gîtes forestiers* in Sore (7) and Pissos (20).

TOURIST OFFICES

Mont de Marsan. 22 rue Victor-Hugo (☎ 58.75.38.67).
La Teste. Pl. J.-Hameau (☎ 56.66.45.59).
Arcachon. Pl. F.-Roosevelt (☎ 56.83.01.69).

MARAIS POITEVIN, VAL DE SÈVRE ET VENDÉE

Region: POITOU

This is the most complicated and least known of the 32 nature parks in France. On the west coast, it is divided into four sectors roughly north and east of La Rochelle and west, east and south of Niort. The main area of 85,000 ha, called the Marais Poitevin, extends due east inland from the Atlantic coast between Esnandes and La Tranche-sur-Mer, with Luçon, Fontenay-le-Comte and Niort on its boundaries. The canals, waterways and rivers of Vendée, Autize, Mignon and Sèvre Niortaise form a major wetland and ornithological reserve. Criss-crossed by duck-weeded canals, this sector has earned the title of *La Venise Verte* (Green Venice). The second area of Mervent Vouvant is north of Fontenay-le-Comte and is an exotic mixture of woods, hills, châteaux, lakes and zoological park. The third area, crescent shaped, is 20 km east of Niort beween St-Maixent and Melles, and contains the forest of Hermitain, dolmens and menhirs, churches, and good walking and riding country. The fourth area is southeast of Niort, heavily wooded with the forests of Chizé and Aulnay. Included in the total park area of 200,000 ha – created in 1975 – are the nature reserves of Pointe d'Arcay on the coast, St-Denis-du-Payré south of Luçon, the Anse d'Aiguillon to the south of the coastal region, and Chizé. Since the sectors are so disparate in physical attributes, flora and fauna, and are separated, it is more practical to treat them as four mini-parks (west, north, east and south.) They are not particularly easy to track down! They all have castles, churches, museums and nature centres to visit. The Benedictine monks from the many abbeys were the first to dig canals in the *marais*, but it was Henri IV's Dutch engineer Humphrey Bradley who finally established the considerable canal network in the early 17thC.

Maps. Michelin 71, 72; IGN 107.

Access. From La Rochelle northeast by N11/N137, east by N11 towards Mauzé-sur-le-Mignon and Niort. From Les Sables-d'Olonne east by

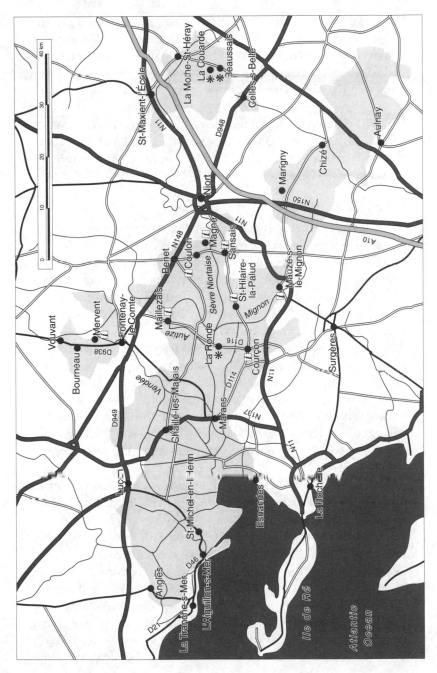

D949 to Luçon, or by D21/D105bis/D46 to L'Aiguillon-sur-Mer. Roads radiate outwards from Niort to the four park areas: the N148 northwest to two park areas, N11 east to another, N150 south to the last. SNCF Paris–Poitiers–Niort and La Rochelle. Plane to La Rochelle-Laleu airport (☎ 46.42.18.27). Many local buses from Niort and La Rochelle.

Park HQ. Maison du Parc, Presbytère, La Ronde, 17170 Courçon (☎ 46.27.82.44). Courçon is halfway between Niort and La Rochelle north of the N11 on the crossroads D114/D116, and La Ronde is a further 8 km north on the D116.

WESTERN AREA

This is the largest and most interesting sector. In the St-Denis-du-Payré ornithological nature reserve southeast of Luçon, west of the D746, it consists of former salt pans, low-lying marshes reclaimed from the sea. Although often flooded in winter, it is a valuable grazing area untouched by fertilisers. Flowers abound including the butterfly iris. Most winters see 4000 duck including 3000 teal, redshank, black-winged stilt, pintail, garganey and black tern nesting on the reserve. Also seen among the reeds, water iris and lilies are glossy ibis, heron, ruff and black-tailed godwit. The water channels are bounded by poplar, willow, alder, ash and tamarisk. Immediately south is the Pointe d'Arcay nature reserve on a large sandbar which has grown southwards across the estuary of the river Lay. The D46 runs along the Atlantic coast from La Tranche-sur-Mer to La Faute-sur-Mer beside the nature reserve. Many mallard, teal, pintail, shoveller, widgeon and shelduck are regular visitors and occasionally brent and greylag geese, spoonbill and avocet. There are wading birds galore – Kentish plover, dunlin, grey plover, curlew and various godwits. In summer hoopoe and shrike can be seen among the maritime pines and scrubby heathland. The third reserve lies immediately south. The Anse de l'Aiguillon is north of La Rochelle, east of the Ile de Ré, and into it come the Marais de la Sèvre waters. The marshy vegetation attracts wildfowl on a huge scale. Ducks number 30–40,000 and waders 50–100,000 including 4000 avocet, 6000 pintail, 6000 shelduck, 20,000 dunlin and 5–20,000 knot plus wild goose, curlew and turnstone. Birds of prey include marsh harrier and kestrel. The shy nocturnal *ragondin* (nutria) also lurks in the marshes together with a multitude of fish and oysters. Migrating and passage species may number 100,000 and wintering birds another 100,000. Round this marvellous series of bird sanctuaries are informa-tion centres at Luçon, 11 pl. Gen.-Leclerc (☎ 51.56.36.52); St-Michel-en-l'Herm, 2 rue de l'Église (☎ 51.30.22.03); L'Aiguillon-sur-Mer, ave. de l'Amiral Courbet (☎ 51.56.42.62); La Faute-sur-Mer, pl. du Rond Point Fleuri (☎ 51.56.45.19); Angles, Mairie (☎ 51.97.56.39) and inland at Marans, 62 rue d'Aligre (☎ 46.01.12.87) and Chaillé-les-Marais, Mairie (☎ 51.56.72.98). Apart from birdwatching in the *marais desséchés* from the flat-bottomed punts called *plates*, you should visit Luçon and St-Michel-en-l'Herm, which have churches of note. Also the *château-musée*, *parc floral* of Court d'Aron at St-Cyr on the D85 west of Luçon should be seen.

At Esnandes across from the Pointe de l'Aiguillon is the Maison de la Myticulture (*moules marinières*) (☎ 46.01.32.13), which doubles as a biology museum and information centre. It is reached southwest from Marans by minor roads.

There are *centres équestres* near Luçon, and sailing, swimming and walking are also popular. Marans offers boating cruises, sailing, swim-ming and horse-drawn *calèches* to explore the countryside. Most of the boats are flat bottomed for obvious reasons.

La Venise Verte runs inland for 40 km from Marans towards Niort and covers an immense network of canals, rivers, streams, marshes, islands, *bocage* and some pastureland. The best places for boat trips are Arcais, Coulon, Magné, La Garette and St-Hilaire-la-Palud.

The birdlife is unspectacular, but fish are abundant, including a rare baby eel called *civelle* which comes from the Sargasso sea. Rosy is the name of the leader of a small otter (*loutre*) colony. Both *civelles* and *loutres* are being carefully protected by the park authorities. There are many aquatic sports available in the half dozen villages which sur-round Green Venice. Other points of interest are the Maison des Marais Mouillés and the aquarium/museum at Coulon. Attractive churches are at Coulon, Magné and Benet and there are two old abbeys: St-Vin-cent at Nieul-sur-l'Autize and St-Pierre at Maillezais. Horses for riding and *calèches* can be hired at St-Hilaire-la-Palud. Information centres are at Coulon-Magné-Sansais, pl. du Colombier (☎ 49.35.99.29); Mauzé-sur-le-Mignon, Mairie (☎ 49.26.30.35); Maillezais, Mairie (☎ 51.00.75.18); St-Hilaire-la-Palud, Mairie (☎ 49.35.32.15); and Courçon, Mairie (☎ 46.01.60.50).

NORTHERN AREA

The smaller northern sector of the park, reached by D938 north from Fontenay-le-Comte, is heavily wooded, with the Forêt de Mervent-Vouvant and château of La Citardière; other châteaux are in Vouvant and Bourneau, and a ruined one with good views is on top of Mont Mervent. Near the Barrage de Mervent is the small Parc-Zoo du Gros Roc and a little further north the Grotte de Père Montfort. The river Vendée, running from north to south, is an attractive feature of the park. Just east of the forest is the Parc Ornithologique de Pagnolle, 2 km away from the Parc-Zoo.

There are information centres at the Château de Mervent (☎ 51.00.20.97) and at fortified Vouvant, pl. de la Mairie (☎ 51.00.80.15). This interesting area has many attractions concentrated into a small area. There are four marked walks, cycles for hire at Bourneau, the Musée du Bois to see in Mervent and the Tour Mélusine in Vouvant, which is reputed to be one of the most beautiful villages in France.

EASTERN AREA

The eastern sector 20 km east of Niort, reached by N11 or D948, is heavily wooded, although unfortunately the A10 slices through its centre. The northwest area, through which the river Sèvre Niortaise runs, is a wide strip south of St-Maixent-l'École, with good walks and a *centre équestre* at Verrière. To the southeast is a larger triangular area with the extensive Forêt Domaniale de l'Hermitain, where wild boar, red deer and roe deer roam. The Sèvre Niortaise runs through it past the château of La Villedieu-de-Comblé, the Château Orangerie at La Mothe-St-Héray and various dolmens to Exouden. There is an information centre at La Mothe-St-Heray, pl. Clemenceau (☎ 49.05.01.41), plus two Maisons du Parc at La Couarde and Beaussais. The small Maison du Protestantisme museum is at La Couarde.

Further southeast across the rivers Lambon and Belle is the southern strip with the abbey of Notre-Dame-de-Celles-sur-Belle, the Château de Chailie and the churches of Verrines-sur-Celles and St-Romans-lès-Melle. A multi-activity sports centre is on the river Lambon 4 km north of Celles-sur-Belle, which has an information centre in pl. de la Poste (☎ 49.79.80.17). The railway and D948 run eastwards from Niort through the park and out to Melle, which has a Huguenot museum, old buildings and, on the outskirts, an old mine in working order, the Château des Ouches and the Tour de Melzéat.

SOUTHERN AREA

The southern sector is 16 km south of Niort with the A10, N150 and railway cutting through it on their way to St-Jean-d'Angély. At the western end is Mauzé-sur-le-Mignon on the N11, with sporting facilities and tourist office. The château of Olbreuse lies 9 km east on the D101 following the river Mignon into the huge forest of Chizé. In the centre at Villiers-en-Bois is the Musée des Insectes et des Papillons (butterfly breeding centre) and the Zoorama Europeén (☎ 49.09.60.04) which has 600 animals, including *baudet* (see below), in a 25 ha park. The deciduous trees include oak, beech, hornbeam, maple, hazel and some plantations of conifer, through which wild boar and deer roam. At the north edge of the forest of Chizé near Marigny on the D102 is the Parc Ornithologique (☎ 49.32.65.35), which has 400 bird species in 2 ha (Apr.–Oct.). At the southern edge of the park are the châteaux of Villeneuve-la-Comtesse and Dampierre-sous-Boutonne. Also a curiosity! The Maison du Baudet du Poitou at La Tillauderie on the D115 is an *Asinerie Expérimentale*, i.e. an ass-breeding centre intent on preserving the medieval species of *baudet*, a unique shaggy donkey.

The Grande Randonnée 36 literally encircles the forest of Chizé and its southeast neighbours the Forêt d'Aulnay and Forêt de Chef-Boutonne. The nearest information centre is just outside the northeast corner at Chef-Boutonne, in the handsome Château de Javarzay (☎ 49.29.80.04).

WHERE TO STAY

There are many campsites within the four sectors of the park, particularly at Nieul-sur-l'Autize, Maillé, Le Mazeau, Vouillé-les-Marais, Coulon, Marans and Champagné-les-Marais. There are holiday villages at Vouillé-la-Taillée, Coulon, Suzé-Vaussais, Marigny and Vouvant. Places to stay with good restaurants are at Arcais, Bessines, Coulon, Damvix, Magné, Maillezais and Le Vanneau.

REGIONAL VISITS

Niort. To see Eleanor of Aquitaine's 12thC fortress-keep, Hôtel de Ville (Le Pilori), covered market, 15thC church of Notre-Dame and museums of Beaux-Arts and Natural History. A tourist train chugs around the town.

Fontenay-le-Comte. A Renaissance town of charm with the château of Terre-Neuve, the clock tower of the church of Notre-Dame, museums and boat trips on the river Vendée.

Surgères. A fortified 13thC town with two châteaux, the 15thC church of St-Pierre and entomological museum.

La Rochelle. A huge city enfranchised by Eleanor of Aquitaine in 1199 with interesting old town and port, 18thC cathedral and seven museums. The Ile de Ré is reached across an isthmus by the N735 or by boat from La Paluce. It was owned alternately by the French and English between the 12thC and 17thC.

PN Pyrénées-Occidentales – Top: Ibex   Below: Chamois

PNR de la Brenne – Top: A medieval fish lake
Below: A European pond tortoise or *cistude*

PNR Brière – Top: Punts or *blins* on the *marais*
Below: Flowers of the wetlands and a picturesque stone-built *gîte*

PNR Haute Vallée de Chevreuse – Top: Chateau de Coubertin
Below: PNR Marais du Cotentin et Du Bessin The traditional flat-bottomed
boats of the *marais* and a view of the region from the air

Plounéour-Ménez. Halfway between Huelgoat and Morlaix is the 12thC Cistercian abbey of Relecq in process of restoration, set beside a lake with mill and fountains.

Brasparts south of St-Rivoal has a large crafts colony of 250 people working and selling their wares at the foot of Mont-St-Michel-de-Brasparts.

St-Hernot. Near Crozon is the Maison des Minéraux (☎ 98.27.19.73), 1030–1900 June–Sept., 1400–1730 Oct.–May. Fee. A permanent exhibition of the region's minerals.

Camaret-sur-Mer. The naval museum portrays the history of Breton fishermen and corsairs and the popular traditions of the area. See also the Fort de Gouin in Camaret-sur-Mer.

Huelgoat has a large pretty lake and gigantic boulders in neighbouring woods.

Breton activities. In the summer months every town and most villages have *animations*, which range from *Fest-Noz* (*fêtes* with dancing), *soirées folkloriques, danses bretonnes, jeux bretons* (often old-fashioned wrestling) to a *festival de musique bretonne* (with traditional instruments such as *bombardes*). Traditional *pardons* (a mixture of religious ceremony and folk festival) take place at Pleyben, La Feuillé, Scrignac, Sizun, Huelgoat and a score of other places. At Molène, Roscanvel and Ouessant religious *bénédictions de la mer* are held when the sea and its rich fish harvests are blessed. There is a highly concentrated range of social, religious, ecological and sporting events held from June–late Sept. On arrival ask at tourist offices or Park HQ.

WHERE TO STAY

There are a dozen small towns with good-value hotels and restaurants offering Breton fare. From west to east: Camaret-sur-Mer, Crozon, Trégarvan, Landévennec, Le Faou-Hanvec, Pont-de-Buis, Brasparts, St-Rivoal, Sizun, Commana, La Feuillée, Huelgoat and Scrignac. Campsites, caravan sites and *gîtes* are to be found in and around the park.

TOURIST OFFICES

Camaret. Quai Toudouze (☎ 98.27.93.69).
Argol (☎ 98.27.77.69).
Brasparts (☎ 98.81.41.25).
Le Huelgoat. Pl. Mairie (☎ 98.99.72.32).
Le Faou. Rue Gén.-de-Gaulle (☎ 98.81.06.85).
Sizun. Pl. Abbé-Broch (☎ 98.68.88.40).
Note: many small offices are open only mid-June–mid-Sept.

TWINNING

The Parc d'Armorique is twinned with the Welsh Pembrokeshire Coast National Park Authority, c/o Upton Castle, Milford Haven Waterway, Dyfed.

REGIONAL VISITS

Brittany also has three notable nature reserves out of a total of 19 around the coast.

Cap Sizun. Established in 1958, this reserve is north of Audierne on the way to the Pointe du Raz. The reserve consists of two areas (offshore) with protected guillemots, puffins, kittiwakes, cormorants, herring gulls, razorbills, ravens and petrels. 1000–1200, 1400–1800 15 Mar.–31 Aug. Information from Faculté des Sciences, ave. le Gorgeu, 29200 Brest (☎ 98.70.13.53).

Les Sept Iles. Established in 1976, this reserve lies 7 km north of the coast east of Roscoff and trips can be booked through Les Vedettes Blanches boat tours (June–Sept.) from Perros-Guirec (☎ 96.23.22.47). Of the seven uninhabited islands only Ile aux Moines can be visited, but Rouzic, Malban and Cerf are interesting to view from the sea. The reserve is managed by LFP, BP 263, La Corderie Royale, 17305 Rochefort. The protected area is 4000 ha and species of nesting seabird include 6000 gannets and fulmars, shag, kittiwake, storm petrel, herring gull, tern, puffin and guillemot. Unfortunately two oil-tanker disasters in 1967 and 1978 polluted and destroyed half the puffin population. Land birds to be seen include linnets, ravens, starlings, kestrels, blackbirds, wrens, greenfinches and rock pipits.

Cap Fréhel. A rocky promontory with two offshore islets, Amas du Cap and La Fauconnière, comprise the Cap Fréhel reserve, near the famous Fort la Latte on the northern Breton coast northwest of St-Castle-Guildo. There are no restrictions on seeing the 300 ha of grasslands and wild moors on the promontory (guided summer walks) and 30 m high cliffs with breeding seabird colonies – herring gull, shag, puffin, fulmar, kittiwake and raven. The lighthouse is the key landmark with Pointe du Jas to the west and Pointe de la Teignouse to the east. The marvellous Grande Randonnée 34 covers most of the Breton coast including Cap Fréhel – ideal for active ornithologists.

NORMANDIE-MAINE

Region: NORMANDY/LOIRE

Founded in 1975, this park covers 234,000 ha and has 151 communes with 90,000 inhabitants. Alençon is the main town, just outside the park but almost surrounded by it. The park is spread over four *départements*, Manche, Mayenne, Orne and Sarthe, so it is partly in Lower Normandy and partly in the northern Loire region. It is forested with over 45,000 ha of woodlands, few hills, of which the highest is 417 m, and is typical Norman *bocage* country with thick, high hedgerows. It is watered by the rivers Mayenne and Varenne to the west, Sarthe to the south, and Cance and Udon to the north towards Caen. There are a number of attractive small towns. In the north Barenton, Domfront, La Ferté-Macé, Carrouges and Sées; Le Mêle-sur-Sarthe in the east; and Sillé-le-Guillaume in the south. In World War II a savage tank battle was fought between the French 2nd Armoured Division and the German 7th Army 12 km southwest of Sées at La Croix-de-Médavy. Agriculture, particularly cattle breeding, cider and perry making, and forestry are the most important occupations in the park. There are plenty of activities, plenty to see and an interesting spa town, Bagnoles-de-l'Orne, where you can take the cure and gamble at the casino. The Norman cuisine is, as you might expect, rather good. Try *andouillette d'Alençon, tripes de la Ferté-Macé,* or *boudin blanc d'Essai* washed down with local cider from Carrouges or perry from Barenton. Travelling is easy. The D907/D908 from Barenton leads eastwards for 80 km via Domfront, La Ferté-Macé and Carrouges to Sées. From Sées the N138 heads south towards Alençon. The southern sector has several good local roads including the D310 and D16.

Maps. Michelin 59, 60; IGN 1719.

Access. North from Le Mans by the N138. From Paris and Dreux westwards by the N12. South from Caen or Rouen by N158 or N138. There are SNCF stations at Alençon, Sées, Pré-en-Pail, La Ferté-Macé, Bagnoles-de-l'Orne and Beaumont. Buses travel frequently between the dozen *villes-portes* of the park.

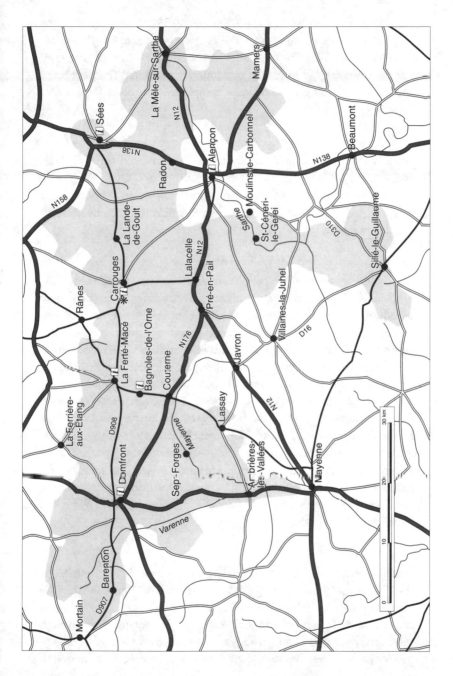

Park HQ. Maison du Parc, Le Chapitre, BP 5, 61320 Carrouges (☎ 33.27.21.15). It is situated near the château and is open 0830–1230, 1330–1730 Mon.–Fri. The building was once used by the château clergy and now has art, folklore, flora and fauna exhibitions. The park management is running an ecological campaign to protect local *bocage* hedgerows.

FAUNA

Woodland species include wild boar, red deer and red squirrel. Altogether there are 1000 deer in the forests of the park. Over 200 species of bird have been noted including buzzards, green woodpeckers, wagtails, warblers, chaffinches, robins and blackbirds. Freshwater fish are abundant.

FLORA AND VEGETATION

Nearly 20 per cent of the park surface (45,200 ha) is wooded. Oak, beech and pine predominate with some spruce and hazel, but many woodland areas are now planted with conifers. The Forêt des Andaines, in addition to magnificent oaks, has chestnuts, beeches and aspens. Wild flowers abound, including orchids. The Association Faune et Flore de l'Orne, 16 rue Étoupée, Alençon (☎ 33.26.26.62) arranges many talks and botanical visits.

The Forêt d'Écouves (1500 ha) is north of Alençon; Perseigne (9000 ha) is southeast; Sillé (8000 ha) is southwest; Monnaye, Andaines and Lande Pourrie are northwest. Each forest has marked walks, e.g. 4 km in Écouves. Visit the Arboretum, Étoile-d'Andaines.

Several valleys and river gorges are worth a visit: the Varenne and Mayenne in the west; the Udon and Cance in the north; and the Sarthe in the south from Alençon towards Sillé crossing the *Alpes Mancelles*, which are 250 m high!

WHAT TO DO

Walks. Consult the Park HQ or Fédération Ornaise de Randonnée, 60 rue St-Blaise, Alençon. The Grandes Randonnées 22 and 36 cross the park. The GR 22 comes in from the east into the Forêt de Perseigne, crosses the river Sarthe and the N12, goes to Radon and west through the Forêt d'Écouves to Carrouges, and runs through the Forêts de Monnaye and des Andaines (with the GR 22B heading northwest), north of Domfront, west through the Forêt de Lande Pourrie and out of the park. The GR 36 arrives in the southwest at Sillé, goes through the Forêt de Sillé, runs north across rivers, meets the GR 22 in the Forêt d'Écouves and continues northwest, keeping east of Carrouges, to leave the park. Ask about the derivatives 36A, B, C and 22A, B, C.

Horse-riding. Every small town has a *centre équestre* and there are nearly 100 km of *sentiers balisés* in the park. Ask at Park HQ for a list or try Village du Cheval, St-Michel-des-Andaines (☎ 33.37.12.79) (north of Bagnoles-de-l'Orne).

Canoe/kayak. Rental from villages along the rivers Varenne, Mayenne and Sarthe, such as St-Léonard-les-Bois, Moulins-le-Carbonnel, Ambrières-les-Vallées, Torchamp and Sept-Forges.

Climbing. *Escalades* at La Fosse-Arthour near St-Georges-de-Rouelley and Les Toyères near St-Pierre-des-Nids. More experienced climbers should try La Roche-au-Loup, Mont-Gérome and Rocher-Broutin in the Forêt des Andaines; Le Saut-de-Cerf and La Roche-Brune in the Forêt d'Écouves; and, in the Forêt de Sillé, the rocks of La Montjoie and L'Aiguillette near Mortain.

Sailing. Étang du Defais north of Sillé-le-Guillaume; Le Mêle-sur-Sarthe in the northeast of the park; and Ambrières-les-Vallées 23 km south of Domfront.

Cycling/VTT. Rental from most SNCF stations including Alençon, Argentan and Flers.

Sports centre. At the Moulin de la Varenne at Torcham (west side) activities include canoe/kayak, climbing, cycle tours and local walks. Ask Park HQ for details.

Roulottes. Horse-drawn caravans for hire (☎ 33.29.00.48 or 33.38.27.78). They hold four people and are usually rented weekly. Full instructions given on equine maintenance!

Discovery walks. Park HQ has devised a dozen *circuits de découverte*

177

including Forges du Champ de la Pierre; Moulins-le-Carbonnel; La Ferrière-aux-Étangs; La Lande de Goult; and St-Céneri-le-Gerei village, said to be one of the 100 prettiest in France. Ask Park HQ for details.

WHAT TO SEE

Châteaux. Domfront (11thC) on hillside overlooking the town; Sillé-le-Guillaume northwest of Le Mans; Lassay northeast of Mayenne has historic pageants; Essay northeast of Alençon; St-Martin-des-Landes south of Carrouges; Couternes near Bagnoles; Rânes northwest of Carrouges; and Château d'O northwest of Sées.

Churches. Sées, 12–14thC Gothic cathedral of Notre-Dame; Alençon, 14–15thC Flamboyant Gothic church of Notre-Dame; Domfront, Romanesque Benedictine Notre-Dame-sur-l'Eau near the river; Sillé-le-Guillaume; St-Céneri-Gerei; Lonlay, abbey.

Museums
Alençon. Musée des Beaux-Arts et de la Dentelle (lace), closed Tue.
Dompierre. Musée de la Mine et des Métiers Anciens (folklore), p.m. only.
Barenton. Musée de la Pomme et de la Poire, closed Mon.
Domfront. Musée Municipal in Mairie (paintings, arms, history).
La Ferté-Macé. Musée Municipal in Hôtel de Ville (paintings, history).
Sées. Musée d'Art et Folklore and Musée Départemental (*beaux-arts*).

Spa town. Bagnoles-de-l'Orne southwest of La Ferté-Macé on the D916 is a spa, with baths, lake, parks, casino, smart hotels and restaurants.

Pear and perry tour. La Route du Poiré starts from Barenton (west side), Maison de la Pomme et de la Poire, and visits four perry makers to the southeast. Allow several hours. There are 25 producers in the park: ask HQ for the list.

WHERE TO STAY

There are 28 campsites, six youth hostels, three *gîtes d'étape* and scores of *gîtes ruraux*. Lists from tourist offices or Park HQ. All of the 13 *villes-portes* on the approaches have a range of hotels to suit all pockets.

178

The most interesting or attractive towns are Bagnoles, Sées, Domfront and Sillé-le-Guillaume.

TOURIST OFFICES

Alençon. Maison d'Ozé (☎ 33.26.11.36).
Domfront. Rue Dr-Barrabé (☎ 33.38.53.97).
Sées. Pl. Gén.-de-Gaulle (☎ 33.28.74.79).
La Ferté-Macé. 13 rue Victoire (☎ 33.37.10.97).
Bagnoles-de-l'Orne. Pl. de la Gare (☎ 33.37.05.84).

CHEVREUSE

Region: ILE-DE-FRANCE

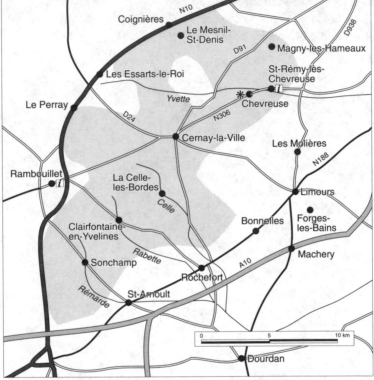

Rather surprisingly, just outside the southwest suburbs of Paris lies the Parc Naturel Régional de la Vallée de Chevreuse, in the area called Île-de-France. Created in spring 1984, it covers 25,600 ha including 10,000 ha of forest with 19 communes and 37,500 inhabitants. Situated in the *département* of Yvelines, it has the Chartres–Paris A10 autoroute on the southern border, the town and forest of Rambouillet to the west, St-Quentin-en-Yvelines to the northeast and Montfort l'Amaury to the northwest. It is watered by the rivers Yvette, Celle, Rabette, Redon and Rémarde. There is a pleasant mixture of woods, valleys, lakes, rivers and fields of wheat, with many interesting walks. But it is still the most urban of the regional parks with a thousand buildings, although abbeys, châteaux, manor houses, windmills and old farmhouses are included in these.

Maps. Michelin 237; IGN 103, 402, 2215.

Access. Roads from Paris include N306, N10, D91. From Dreux east-wards is the N12. From Chartres heading northeast is the D906, and from Étampes westwards is the N191/N10. The A10 exit is at Dourdan. SNCF stations from Paris (Montparnasse) are Rambouillet, Le Perray and La Maison-Neuve.

Park HQ. Maison du Parc, Château de la Madeleine, 78460 Chevreuse (☎ 30.52.09.09). Reached by the N306 from Rambouillet or D938 from Versailles. Free maps and leaflets available. Open Mon.–Fri. 1000–1200, 1400–1800.

FAUNA

The only significant wildlife is to be seen in the Parc Animalier des Yvelines, 78120 Sonchamp (☎ 34.84.51.21). Run by the Office National des Forêts, it is open Sat. 1300–1800, Sun. and public holidays 0800–1800. Fee. Access is by D27 east of Rambouillet on the way to Clairfon-taine-en-Yvelines. Wild boar, stags, roe deer and fallow deer roam in their natural habitat. Freshwater fish abound in rivers and lakes. Taking of photographs allowed only on Tue.

FLORA

In the many forests and woods (Yvelines, Angervilliers, St-Arnoult, Maréchaux, Vindrins, etc.) are beech, oak, sweet chestnut and some lime trees but no flowers of note.

LAKES

Several of the lakes are quite spectacular, especially the Étang de la Tour des Noés in the Forêt des Yvelines, Cernay near the old abbey of Les Vaux de Cernay, and Roches near Dampierre.

WHAT TO DO

Walks. Within the park there are 17 km of signed walks, designated by red-and-white flashes. The Grande Randonnée 1 from Rambouillet through the Forêt des Yvelines heads east and then south to St-Arnoult-en-Yvelines through the Forêt de St-Arnoult towards Dourdan. The GR 11 arrives at Coignières in the northwest of the park and runs southeast past Le Mesnil-St-Denis alongside the river Yvette to Chevreuse. Here it branches south of the river (one way through the woods around Choisel and the other past the Château de Coubertin and south) and links up again at Les Molières, runs due south to Forges-les-Bains and Machery and heads for the Château du Marais. Another walk is the Chemin Jean-Racine from Chevreuse to Port-Royal due north through woods past churches and châteaux to the Abbaye de Port-Royal-des-Champs (15 km there and back). The RER station of St-Remy-lès-Chevreuse makes a convenient start point ☎ (1) 545.31.02 for local information on walks.

Horse-riding. There are 13.5 km of marked bridleways in the park and five *centres équestres*: Le Club des Peupliers, Chevreuse; Bonnelles, on rte du Bullion; Centre de St-Léger-en-Yvelines; Haras de la Gire at Levis-St-Nom; also in Perray-en-Yvelines. Five- or seven-day *stages* (courses) are offered at special prices including lodging.

Canoe-kayak. Centre de St-Quentin-en-Yvelines (☎ 30.58.36.51) and Centre Municipale Apay, square Kennedy, Rambouillet (☎ 36.46.82.48).

Swimming. At Chevreuse, Rambouillet (Étang d'Or), St-Arnoult-en-Yvelines (lake), St-Quentin-en-Yvelines (*base nautique*).

WHAT TO SEE

Musée National des Granges de Port-Royal. 78470 Magny-les-Hameaux (☎ 30.43.73.05). Reached by D91/D46 north of Chevreuse. Open 1000–1130, 1430–1730. Closed Mon.–Tue. Fee. Historical background of Port-Royal and the Jansenist religious movement.

Musée des Ruines de l'Abbaye de Port-Royal-des-Champs. Address as above (300 m away) (☎ 30.43.74.93). Same hours. Fee.

182

Château de Breteuil. 78460 Choisel (☎ 30.52.05.02). Access by D40 southwest from Chevreuse. The château dates from the reign of Henri IV and is usually open 1430–1730 but all day in July–Aug. Fee. The park of 70 ha is open 1000–1700.

Château de Dampierre. 78720 Dampierre-en-Yvelines (☎ 30.52.53.24). Lies west of Chevreuse on the D58. Open 1400–1800 Apr.–Oct. Fee. Built by Mansart in the 17thC, it consists of three large buildings with grey slate roofs in a quadrangle. The gardens were designed by Le Nôtre and it is possible to fish in the lakes.

Château de la Madeleine in Chevreuse. Open 1400–1800 Mon., Fri., Sat., Sun. 1000–1200, 1400–1800. Fee. A medieval fortress partly destroyed by Richelieu, it still has a height of 80 m and overlooks the town.

Other châteaux, which can be seen only from the outside include: Château le Mesnil-St-Denis east of Coignières, Château Senlisse in Parc de Dampierre, Château de Coubertin on the outskirts of St-Remy-lès-Chevreuse, and Château du Marais on D27 west of Brevillet. Château Bandeville and Château Rochefort are between Dourdan and St-Arnoult, and Château les Bordes is northwest of Bullion.

WHERE TO STAY

Gîte d'Étape des Hauts-Besnières, Maison des Hauts-Besnières, La Hogue, 78720 La Celle-les-Bordes, on the N306 east of Rambouillet, is ideal for walkers. Two other *gîtes d'étape* are at Bonnelles (☎ 30.41.47.18) and just north of Rambouillet (☎ 34.83.83.09). Also the Maison de For, Vaux-de-Cernay, Dampierre, is a new *relai*. Hotels are in Dourdan (pop. 8000), Senlisse village, Rambouillet (pop. 22,500) and Versailles (pop. 95,000). There are youth hostels in Mantes-la-Jolie and Oinville-Meulan. Campsites are at Bois d'Arcy (St-Quentin-en-Yvelines), Les Bréviaries, Le Perray-en-Yvelines, Rambouillet and St-Arnoult-en-Yvelines.

TOURIST OFFICES

St-Rémy-lès-Chevreuse, opposite Gare RER, 1 rue Ditte (☎ 30.52.22.49). Rambouillet. Hôtel de Ville (☎ 34.83.21.21).

MARAIS DU COTENTIN ET DU BESSIN

Region: NORMANDY

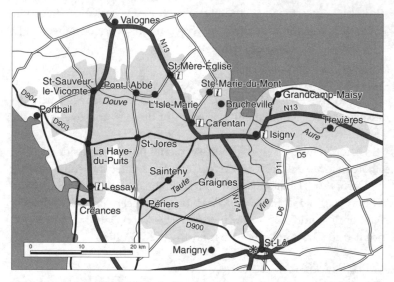

The Parc Naturel Régional des Marais du Cotentin et du Bessin, created in 1991, covers 113,000 ha and contains 108 communes with 57,000 inhabitants in the *départements* of Manche and Calvados. The region is mainly *marais* marshlands, peat bogs, polders and *bocages*. On the west coast is the Havre (haven) de Lessay, and on the east coast the Baie des Veys and the famous World War II invasion beaches of Utah and Omaha. The only town of significance is Carentan (pop. 7000) in the centre, and the most important villages are Lessay, La Haye-du-Puits, St-Sauveur-le-Vicomte, L'Isle Marie, Périers, Ste-Mère-Église, Brucheville and Isigny-sur-Mer. The park's northern boundary is south of Valognes (21 km from Cherbourg), its southern boundary runs north of St-Lô where the Park HQ is sited, and in the east the park ends to the west of Bayeux. The park is crammed with a dozen rivers (among them the Douve, Aure, Vire and Taute), canals (Espagnols and Vire et Taute) and many forests (Cerisy in the southeast, Hommet in the centre,

184

Landes de Lessay, La Lande, Mont Castre, St-Sauveur and others in the western sector). There are five protected reserves. On the east coast is Ste-Marie-du-Mont and Pointe de Brévands; in the centre Roselière-des-Rouges-Pièces and two *marais* in the northwest, La Sangeurièrc and L'Adriennerie. The bird life is interesting and extensive; there are a score of small châteaux/manor houses, half a dozen museums, good walks, boat rides and ornithological tours. There is also a funny little tourist train which chugs between Carentan and the west, plus the usual campsites and *gîtes*. Farming and fishing are main activities and the Norman cuisine is rich and satisfying.

Maps. Michelin 54; IGN 6.

Access. South from Cherbourg by N13 to Carentan or D904 southwest to Lessay and La Haye-du-Puits. West from Bayeux by N13. Northwest by D900, north by N174 or northeast by D6/D11 from St-Lô. The SNCF between Cherbourg and Bayeux stops at Carentan. Country buses ply between Bayeux, St-Lô and Cherbourg.

Park HQ. Maison du Département, Rond-Point de la Liberté, 50008 St-Lô (☎ 33.05.97.72). St-Lô is 28 km southeast of Carentan with a population of 25,000 and half a dozen *auberges* and good restaurants.

FAUNA

In the forests there are deer, squirrels, fox and minor wildlife, but bird species are prolific since the park is on the major migration axis between Scandinavia and Africa: in particular heron, grey curlew, shelduck, buzzard, grebe, snipe, pintail duck, eider duck and corn-crake. In the Havre de Lessay on the west coast and Baie des Veys on the east coast, in addition to curlew and duck there are geese and oyster-catchers (*huitriers-pies*) In typical *marais* such as St-Clair expect to see finches, wrens, spring wagtails and wheatear stonechats. In the canals there are eels, watersnakes and a wide variety of fish, frogs, etc. Butterflies are everywhere in early summer. There is an ornithological reserve west of Omaha Beach.

FLORA AND VEGETATION

In the Forêt de Cerisy are oak and beech, and there are conifers in the

185

minor woods near sand-dunes and canals. Broom, heather, reeds, sedge, osier and willow are to be seen in the wetlands. Huge hedgerows, many of them centuries old, still mark the boundaries of the *bocage* country: a major hazard to the invading Allied troops in the summer of 1944. Local peasants still blend strips of marsh bushes into *lanières* to form *rôtz* as roof thatch or to cover their apple presses, since this is calvados and cider country. In 400 ha of La Sangsurière *marais* 122 flower/shrub species, including the yellow *pygamon*, have been identified.

WHAT TO DO

Walks. The Grande Randonnée 223 comes down the west coast from Cherbourg, past Cap de la Hague, Carteret, Lessay and inland south of St-Lô. The park authorities have marked some 2½ km of trails around the Havre de Lessay bay and the sand-dunes on the west side of the village of Créances. Other local marked walks start from Marchésieux and St-Martin d'Aubigny.

Boat trips. From Embarcadère de Jourdan (N13 north of Carentan) and St-Sauveur-le-Vicomte (northwest) boats, canoes and kayaks can be hired to cruise along the rivers Douve and Seve.

Swimming. There are half a dozen beaches on the west coast between Carteret and Lessay, with beach villas for summer rental, and on the east coast where the Americans landed on Utah and Omaha in 1944.

Horse-riding. There is a Hippodrome at Graignes 6 km south of Carentan, where you can hire horses, rent a five-place *roulotte*-caravan or ride in a 15-seater horse-drawn *chariot bâché* (☎ 33.41.38.75).

Cycling/VTT. Cycles can be hired in St-Lô and Carentan. Ask at SNCF or tourist offices.

Train ride. On summer weekends an elderly but safe train will take you between Carentan and Baupte, 8 km west, to explore the *marais* (☎ 33.42.74.01).

Courses. Ecological *stages* are held during the summer months at weekends (☎ 31.95.11.89). For children 12–15 years for two weeks, *marais* on foot or by canoe, bike or train. Campsite (☎ 33.05.68.04).

Nature visits. Ornithological and botanical visits are arranged by the Park HQ throughout the year starting from Brévands, Doville, Carentan, Trevières, Lessay, Marchésieux and Ste-Marie-du-Mont to see reserves at Beauguillot, La Sangsurière, Tourbière de Mathon, Marais de l'Aure and Baie des Veys (☎ 31.43.52.56 or 31.95.11.89 or 33.05.68.04). Small fee.

WHAT TO SEE

Châteaux. There are 28 châteaux/manor houses within the park area. The most interesting are the Château de Colombières, off the D5 halfway between Carentan and Bayeux, closed Tue. p.m.; St-Pierre-de-Mont, east of Grandcamp-Maisy; Pirou, south of Lessay; Château de Montfort near Marchésieux; and Balleroy, halfway between Bayeux and St-Lô off the D572.

Churches. There are a dozen *églises classées* in the park including from west to east St-Germain-sur-Ay, Vesly, Orglandes, Pont-l'Abbé, Picauville, Périers, Auxais, St-Mère-Église, Ste-Marie-du-Mont, Carentan, Marchésieux, Brévands, Gefosse-Fontenay and Vouilly.

Museums. Maison des Marais, Marchésieux off the D900 east of Périers (marshland traditions) July–Aug. p.m. only; Musée de la Vannerie, Remilly-sur-Locon (120 years of wickerworking) June–Sept., closed Sun.; Ferme du Cotentin, Ste-Mère-Église (farm life, folklore) Easter–Sept., closed Tue.; two small museums near Le Molay-Littry, north of the Forêt de Cerisy.

Crafts. Visit to porcelain factory in Ville-d'Isigny-sur-Mer; caramels at La Cambe; 15thC fortified farm at L'Hermerel (☎ 31.22.17.44). Ask Park HQ for details of local craftspeople.

World War II sites. There are two sad but well-kept cemeteries, an American one near Omaha Beach and a German one inland on the N13 on the way to Bayeux. For details of visits to wartime beaches ☎ 31.22.43.08.

WHERE TO STAY

There are 12 campsites, some *gîtes* and small *auberges* in Carentan, Grandcamp-Maisy, Périers, Lessay, La Haye-du-Puits and Isigny-sur-Mer. More sophisticated hotels can be found in Bayeux, St-Lô and Valognes. Ask the tourist offices for campsite and *gîte* details.
Useful addresses:
Pays d'Acceuil du Bessin, Le Molay-Littry (☎ 31.22.17.44).
Vivre en Cotentin, Village de Gîtes, Lessay (☎ 33.46.37.06).
Maison des Marais, Marchésieux (☎ 33.07.15.20).
Association le Fayard, quai à Tangue (☎ 33.05.68.04).

TOURIST OFFICES

Carentan. Mairie (☎ 33.42.74.00).
Isigny. 1 rue Victor-Hugo (☎ 31.21.46.00).
Lessay. Mairie (☎ 33.46.46.18).
Ste-Marie-du-Mont. Mairie (☎ 33.71.58.00).
Ste-Mère-Église. Mairie (☎ 33.21.00.33).

REGIONAL VISITS

World War II beaches Omaha, Gold and Juno on the east coast. Bayeux to see the cathedral and famous tapestry.

BROTONNE

Region: NORMANDY

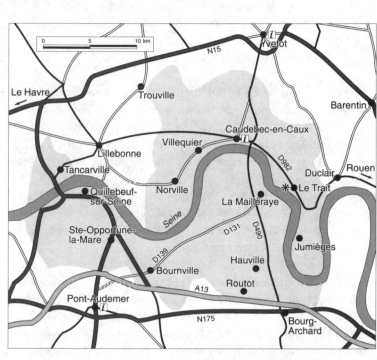

Created in 1974, the regional park of Brotonne covers 42,000 ha spread over 37 communes in the *départements* of Eure and Seine-Maritime. The Haute-Normandie region is near the English Channel and has rich forests, the Brotonne and Maulévrier. The park was conceived as a barrier between the industrial regions of Le Havre and Rouen, and the river Seine, much polluted unfortunately, meanders from the estuary under the Tancarville bridge and winds in serpentine fashion east-wards past Caudebec-en-Caux, Jumièges and Rouen towards Paris. The park is on both sides of the first main loop and consists of four natural regions – Pays de Caux, the Seine valley, the Roumois area and the Marais Vernier area. The park is entirely open to the public except for the wildlife reserve of Mannevilles (☎ 35.91.83.16) in the Marais Vernier. Small towns within the park, which has a total population of

189

33,000, include Caudebec, Jumièges, La Maillèraye-sur-Seine and Le Trait. The economy is based on fruit growing, mainly cider apples and cherries, and beef cattle raising, plus tourism of course. For a number of years the Brotonne was considered to be a 'dull' park with *végétation banale*, but since 1980 introduction of new fauna and flora has been very successful, despite the Seine valley oil refineries.

Maps. Michelin 55; IGN 7, 102, 420.

Access. From the north by D490 crossing the Seine by the Pont de Brotonne. The autoroute A13 thunders from west to east south of the park (Exits 25 and 26). The D131/139 bisects the park from southwest to northeast. The nearest SNCF station is Yvetot on the Paris–Le Havre line. Buses run from Rouen to Pont-Audemer and Le Havre.

Park HQ. Maison du Parc, 2 Rond-point Marbec, 76580 Le Trait (☎ 35.91.83.16/35.37.23.16), 0900–1200, 1400–1900 (the administration centre is closed Sat.–Sun.). Le Trait is on the D982 on the north bank of the Seine between Duclair and Caudebec.

CEDENA. Centre de Découverte de la Nature du Parc Régional de Brotonne, pl. de l'Église, Ste-Opportune-la-Mare, 27680 Quillebeuf-sur-Seine (☎ 32.56.94.87). On the south side of the Marais Vernier, on the D810 8 km north of Pont-Audemer, CEDENA organises a complete annual ecological programme, ideal for children and students, with nature studies, courses, camps, visits and canoe trips. CEDENA has also undertaken scientific and ecological studies of the nature reserve of Mannevilles.

FAUNA

Curiously enough, the most exotic species are Scottish-bred cattle, Shetland sheep and small Camargue horses living free in the Réserve des Mannevilles. CEDENA has produced an inventory of dragonflies (*libellules*). There are wild boar, foxes, deer, rabbits, black storks which can be seen in the *marais* during August, wild geese, heron, teal, duck, swans, and of course Norman cattle everywhere. Buzzards, snipe, woodcock, duck species and curlew have been reintroduced in the last decade.

FLORA AND VEGETATION

In the large woods of Brotonne and Trait-Maulévrier are to be seen beech, chestnut, oak, hornbeam, silver birch and pine, and at La Haye-de-Routot are two immensely old yew trees. Much of the area is marshland with the usual reeds, rushes and fish, eels, frogs and snakes. One peculiar species is the *flora carnivora* of sundew (*drosera*). Also look carefully for the 'burning' lobelia, purple orchid, marsh valerian and royal fern amid the Marais Vernier.

ECOMUSÉE DE LA BASSE-SEINE

The park authorities have recently upgraded the *ecomusée* which comprises six different museums and attracts 100,000 visitors a year.

Le Moulin de Pierre at Hauville near Routot (☎ 32.56.84.93) is a 13thC *monument historique*.

Le Four à Pain at La Haye-de-Routot (☎ 32.57.34.77) is a *musée de la boulangerie,* and there is a separate *atelier* called Musée du Sabotier, which traces the history of sabot/clog making.

La Maison de la Pomme et la Forge at Ste-Opportune-la-Mare (☎ 32.56.94.87), closed Sat.–Sun., is a museum on the history of apple growing and calvados and cider making. Also in Ste-Opportune there is a traditional forge at work on Sun. called **La Forge de Village** (☎ 35.38.15.43).

Le Musée des Métiers at Bourneville (☎ 32.57.40.41), closed Tue., is a folklore and craft museum of the traditional Norman skills of thatching, glassmaking, pottery, ceramics, ironwork, etc.

Le Musée de la Marine de Seine at Caudebec-en-Caux (☎ 35.96.27.30), closed Tue. A museum of the naval and fishing history of the Seine valley with a wide variety of boats and ships to see.

Expect to pay a small entry fee. The smaller museums close in winter. The lighthouse (*phare*) of St-Samson-de-la-Roque and the stone windmill of Hauville are also worth a visit.

WHAT TO DO

Walks. Grande Randonnée 23 crosses the park from west to east between the Marais Vernier and Jumièges. The GR 2 runs along the north bank of the Seine between Tancarville and Le Trait. CEDENA and the Park HQ can suggest a wide variety of nature rambles.

191

Horse-riding. Centre Hippique at Notre-Dame-de-Gravenchon (☎ 35.38.67.96) and Centre Équestre du Parc, Le Fief du Wuy, La Maillèraye-sur-Seine (☎ 35.37.34.46) offer horse-riding activities.

WHAT TO SEE

UCPA. Base de Plein Air et de Loisirs, Jumièges-le-Mesnil (☎ 35.37.93.84), open every day May–Aug., closed Sun. Sept.–Apr. A leisure centre around a large lake with a wide variety of sports available.

Musée Victor-Hugo. Villequier near Caudebec, 1000–1200, 1400–1900 (closed Tue.). Near the banks of the Seine, this little museum commemorates the history of the Hugo family. Fee.

Abbeys. The finest Norman abbey is at Jumièges. Now in ruins, it was founded in the 7thC and rebuilt in the 10thC. There is another 7thC abbey at St-Martin-de-Boscherville .

Lillebonne. A notable Roman theatre, 13thC château, 16thC church and several museums to visit.

Château d'Ételan. Off the D81 near Norville on the north bank of the Seine. Cultural history of Normandy in a fine 19thC restored château.

WHERE TO STAY

All small towns, such as Caudebec, Duclair and Pont-Audemer, and villages for miles around, offer a wide choice of hotels and *auberges* with excellent Norman cuisine and cider. Each tourist office has a list of *gîtes*. Contact ADTER, chemin de la Bretagne, BP 57, 76230 Bois-Guillaume (☎ 35.60.48.60). There is a camping/caravan site Plein-Air at Jumièges, 76480 Duclair. The abbey of St-Wandrille near Caudebec offers religious retreats for people wishing to visit the park.

TOURIST OFFICES

Rouen. 25 pl. de la Cathédrale (☎ 35.71.41.77).
Le Havre. Pl. de l'Hôtel de Ville (☎ 35.21.22.88).
Caudebec. Maison des Templiers, pl. Ch.-de-Gaulle (☎ 35.96.20.65).
Yvetot. Mairie, pl. Victor-Hugo (☎ 35.95.08.40).
Pont-Audemer. Pl. Maubert (☎ 32.41.08.21).

GLOSSARY

FAUNA

Mammals

belette	weasel
blaireau	badger
bouquetin	ibex
campagnol	field vole
castor	European beaver
cerf	stag, hart
cerf commun	red deer
chamois	chamois
chauve-souris	bat
chevreuil	roebuck
coypou	coypu
daim	fallow deer
écureil	squirrel
fouine	stone marten
genette	genet, wildcat
gibier	game
hermine	stoat, ermine
lapin	rabbit
lièvre	hare
loup	wolf
loutre	otter
lynx	lynx
marmotte	marmot
martre	marten
mésange	titmouse
mouflon	wild sheep
mulot	fieldmouse
ours	bear
phoque	seal
putois	polecat
renard, roux	red fox
sanglier	wild boar
taupe	mole
vison	mink

Fish and reptiles

anguille	eel
brème	bream
brochet	pike
carpe	carp
couleuvre	grass-snake
crapaud	toad
écrevisse	crayfish
grenouille	frog
lézard	lizard
omble-chevalier	char
perche	perch
saumon	salmon
serpent	snake
tanche	tench
tortue, terrapin	terrapin
truite	trout
vipère	viper, adder

Birds

aigle royal	golden eagle
aigrette	egret
alouette	lark
autour	goshawk
avocette	avocet
bécasseur	dunlin
bergeronnette	wagtail
bruant	ortolan bunting
busard	harrier, buzzard
buse	buzzard
butor	bittern
canard	duck
canard siffleur	widgeon
chouette	owl
chouette effraie	barn owl
cormoran	cormorant
cormoran huppé	shag
courlis	curlew
crécerelle	kestrel
échassier	wader
faisan	pheasant
faucon pélerin	peregrine falcon
fauvette	warbler
flamant rose	flamingo
foulque	coot
gobeur	gull, seamew
grand corbeau	raven
grand tétras	capercaillie
grèbe	grebe
grive	thrush
harle	merganser
héron	heron

193

hibou	owl
hirondelle	swallow
hirondelle de mer	tern
huppe	hoopoe
lagopède alpin	ptarmigan
loriot	oriole
macareux	puffin
malard	mallard
martin-pêcheur	kingfisher
martinet	swift, martlet
merle	blackbird
merle d'eau	water-ouzel
migrateurs	birds of passage
milan	kite
milouin	pochard
mouette	gull, seamew, kittiwake
nicheur	nester
oie	goose
oiseau de mer	sea bird
perdrix	partridge
pic	woodpecker
pipi	pipit
pluvier	plover
pouillot	willow warbler
poule d'eau	moorhen
pygargue	osprey
rapaces	birds of prey
renouée	knot
sarcelle	teal
souchet	shoveller
tadorne	sheldrake
tétras	grouse

FLORA AND VEGETATION

ajonc	gorse
anémone	anemone
asphodèle	asphodel
bocage	hedgerow, copse (Normandy)
bois	wood
bruyère	heather
campanule	campanula
coquelicot	field poppy
crocus	crocus
cyclamen	cyclamen
édelweiss	edelweiss
ellébore	hellebore
forêt	forest
fougère	bracken
garrigue	evergreen bushes, gorse
gentiane	gentian

iris	iris
jacinthe	hyacinth
jonc à balais	reed
jonc des marais	bulrush
jonquille	daffodil
lis	lily
lobélie	lobelia
maquis	Corsican scrub
marais, marécage	marsh
muguet	lily of the valley
myrica	bog myrtle
myrte	myrtle
narcisse	narcissus
nénuphar	water lily
orchidée	orchid
orchis	wild orchid
pavot	poppy
pied-d'alouette	larkspur
pierce-neige	snowdrop
primevère	primula, cowslip
rhododendron	rhododendron
roselière	reed-bed
rosier des Alpes	alpenrose
saxifrage	saxifrage
tourbière	peat bog
tulipe	tulip
valériane	valerian
violette	violet
vipérine	viper's bugloss

Trees

aulne	alder
bouleau	birch
châtaignier	chestnut
chêne	oak
chêne vert	holm oak
coudrier	hazel
épicéa	Norwegian spruce
figue	fig
frêne	ash
génévrier	juniper
hêtre	beech
hêtre blanc	hornbeam
houx	holly
if	yew
marronier	horse chestnut
olivier	olive
orme blanc	Scotch elm
peuplier	poplar
pin	pine
pin sylvestre	Scotch fir
sapin	fir
saule	willow
tilleul	lime

INDEX

NB: The more common species of flora and fauna are not indexed, but can be found under FLORA or FAUNA in each park.

195

INDEX

INDEX

Guil river 89, 93
Guillestre 89, 92, 93; (park HQ) 91
Guînes forest 5, 8

Haguenau 25
Hanau, étang de 25; botanical reserve 26
hang-gliding 67, 97
harriers 30, 96, 124; marsh 112, 150, 169; Montagu's 54, 169
Hautes-Chaumes 60
Haute-Touche zoo 157
Haut Folin mountain 42, 44, 45
Hautvilliers, Marne 13; abbey 15
Havre, Le 189, 192
Havre de Lessay 184, 185, 186
Haye reserve, Lorraine 19
herons 8, 48, 117, 150, 157, 185; grey 19, 25; purple 19, 112
hoopoes 60, 102, 107, 150
horses; Camargue 190; Przewalski 125
horse-riding see WHAT TO DO in individual parks
Huelgoat 168, 169, 170, 171, 172
Hyéres 109; (park HQ) 107

ibex 1, 2, 72, 77, 78, 96, 137
ibis 150
Ile du Levant 109
Ile Molène 167, 168, 171
Ile d'Ouessant 167, 168, 169, 171
Ile de Porquerolles 109
Isère river 70, 79
Isola 2000 96, 98, 99
Issoir (park HQ) 54

Jumièges 189, 190, 191, 192

kayaks see WHAT TO DO in individual parks
kestrels 8, 54, 102, 150, 172
kites 96; royal 19; red 54, 112
knots 150

Lac d'Allos 94, 98
Lac d'Annecy 82
Lac de Der-Chantecoq 31, 33
Lac Foréant 93
Lac de Grand Lieu 165–6
Lac de Laouzas 129, 132, 133, 134
Lac de la Ravière 129, 132, 134
Lac de Ste-Anne 92
Lachaussée lake 19
Lajoux (park HQ) 48

lakes; (Brenne) 156, 157; (Chevreuse) 181; (Ecrins) 85; (Pilat) 68; (Volcans d'Auvergne) 55–6; (Vosges) 37; see also individual names; étangs
lammergeiers 124
Lans-en-Vercors (park HQ) 71
Lessay 184, 186, 187, 188
lilies; martagon 48, 72, 86, 125; orange 86; St Bruno 96; yellow 131; turk-cap 138
Lindre lake (étang) 17, 19
Lille (park HQ) 7
Loire river 64; valley 160
Lons-le-Saunier 48
Lons-le-Sauveur 51
Lourdes 136, 141
Lubéron mountains 101, 103
Lucon 148, 150, 151
Luz valley 136, 137, 139, 140
Luz-St-Sauveur 136, 139, 140
Luzy 46
lynxes 36, 48, 137

Madine lake 19, 21, 22
Maginot Line 24, 26; museum 27
Maisons du parc see Park HQ in each park
Mannevilles reserve 190
Manosque 102, 103, 104, 105
maps see individual parks
Marans 151
marais (wetlands) 8, 144, 148, 150, 161, 184, 185, 188
Marais du Bout du Lac d'Annecy reserve 82
Marais Vernier 189, 190, 191
Mare à Goriaux, la (lake) 5, 7
marmots 72, 90, 96
Marne river 12
Marquenterre, Parc ornithologique de 8
marshes, salt 20, 21, 118
martens 25, 54, 137, 157, 168; pine 36; stone 25
martins 8; crag 65
Mazamet 129, 130, 132, 133
Maulévrier forest 189, 191
Mayenne river 176, 177
megaliths/menhirs see stones, standing
Melle 152
Mende 123, 124, 126, 128
Ménez-Hom 167, 170
Ménez-Meur (park HQ) 168
Menton 95, 97
mergansers 30, 165

198

Méribel 80, 81
Mervent 152
Metz 17, 19, 20, 23, 25
Meuse river 17
Mézières-en-Brenne 158, 159, 160
Millau 123, 128
mines, silver 39
mink, European 157
Mittersheim lake 17, 21
Modane 78
Mont Aigoual 123, 124, 125, 126
Mont Bar, volcano 62
Mont Beuvray 42, 44
Mont-Dauphin 89, 91
Mont Joli 12
Mont Lozère 123, 124, 125, 126
Mont-de-Marsan 143, 147
Mont Pilat 64, 68
Mont Sinai 12, 15
Mont Vinaigre 106, 108
Montagne de Bouges 123
Montagne Noire 131, 132
Montagne de Ste-Victoire 105
Monts d'Arrée 167, 168
Monts du Cantal 52, 55
Monts Dôme 52, 55
Monts Dore 52, 55
Monts du Forez 58, 61
Monts du Jura 47, 75
Monts du Livradois 58
Montreuil 8
Montsauche-les-Settons 42, 44
Morez 47, 48, 49, 50, 51
Morlaix 167, 168
Moselle river 17
mouflons; (Armorique) 168;
    (Cévennes) 124; (Haut-Languedoc)
    130; (Mercantour) 96; (Pas de C) 7;
    (Pilat) 65; (Vercors) 72; (Volcans
    d'A) 54; (Queyras) 90
moths, Spanish moon 90
Moutiers 78
Munster 35, 36, 37, 38, 39, 40
museums *see* WHAT TO DO in
    individual parks
myrtle 26, 60, 112

Nancy 17, 19, 20, 22–3
Néouvielle nature reserve 135, 137,
    138
Nevers 46
Nice 98; (park HQ) 95
Niederbronn-les-Bains 28
Niort 148, 150, 153
nutria 150, 162

Olliergues 58, 60
Oloron-Ste-Marie 136, 140
orchids; (Brotonne) 191; (Cévennes)
    125; (Corsica) 112; lady's slipper
    72, 79, 86; (Lorraine) 20;
    (Mercantour) 96; Traunstein 26;
    (Volcans d'A.) 54
Orcières 84, 86, 87
orienteering 66
orioles, golden 19, 54, 117
ornithological reserves 8, 51, 117, 118,
    185; (Armorique) 172, 173; La
    Dombes 70; La Teich 142, 144;
    (Forêt d'O) 32; (Marais-Poit.) 148,
    150, 152, 153
ospreys 8, 25, 112
Ossau valley 135, 136, 137, 138, 139
otters 19, 54, 102, 162, 168
ouzels, ring 79
owls 8, 54; barn 25; eagle 96;
    Grand-Duc 72, 102, 130; sparrow
    19; Tengmalm 25, 79, 85, 96
oystercatchers 8, 144, 165

Pagnolle, ornithological park 152
Pannessière lake 42, 44
parish closes (*enclo parois*) 167
Park HQ *see* individual parks
Pélussin 66, 67, 68; (park HQ) 65
Pertuis 102, 104, 105
Petite-Pierre, La 25, 26, 27, 28; (park
    HQ) 25
petrels 8, 172
photography tours 80, 119
Piney (park HQ) 30; wildlife reserve
    32
pintails 150, 165, 185
pipits 8, 117, 172; meadow 60; tree 48
Pissos 145, 146, 147
Plagne, La 79, 80
Plaine de la Scarpe et de l'Escaut 5, 7
Platier d'Oye reserve 8
plovers 8, 116, 117, 144, 150, 165
pochards 7, 19, 48
Pointe d'Arcey nature reserve 148, 150
polecats 8, 54
Pont-Audemer 191, 192
Pont-de-Gau, ornithological park 117
Pont-à-Mousson 17, 19, 20
Pont-en-Royans, hanging houses 75
potholing *see* WHAT TO DO in
    individual chapters
Pra-Loup 97, 99
pratincoles 116
Prémanon 49, 50
ptarmigan 79, 85, 90

INDEX